CHAUCER THE MAKER

CHAUCER THE MAKER

by

JOHN SPEIRS

"In wit and in good reason of sentence he [Chaucer] passeth all other makers."
—T. USK.

"Here all is in life and motion; here we behold the true Poet or Maker."
—JOSEPH WARTON.

FABER AND FABER
24 Russell Square
London

First published in mcmli
by Faber and Faber Limited
24 Russell Square, London W.C.1
First published in this edition mcmlxiv
Reprinted mcmlxvii
Printed in Great Britain by
John Dickens and Co Ltd Northampton
All rights reserved

To
RUTH and LOGAN

ACKNOWLEDGMENTS

A considerable part of the substance of what was to be this book appeared first in *Scrutiny*. This is the place, therefore, to acknowledge my inestimable debt to the work of a great critic, Mr. Leavis and—for invaluable suggestions—to Mrs. Leavis. A more adequate acknowledgment to them would have been a much better book.

This book could not have been carried through without the understanding assistance of my wife, Ruth Speirs.

J. S.

University College,
   Exeter.

CONTENTS

CONTENTS

NOTE ON QUOTATIONS

Though I have assumed that the reader who might be interested in a detailed commentary on Chaucer's poetry will have at hand one of the editions of Chaucer, complete with glossary and some guidance as to pronunciation, I have selected and quoted freely. My own experience has been that quotations often surprisingly bring home to one a realization of how good an author is. It needs to be said again, perhaps, in relation to these quotations, that Chaucer's poetry requires to be listened to; and that listening to Chaucer is not listening to what is often called the 'sound', as we may listen to Spenser, Milton, Tennyson or Swinburne, but is listening to English being spoken. It is very necessary to take some pains to learn how to read Chaucer's poetry aloud or at least to listen with the inner ear to it talking. The pains have been greatly exaggerated. The metre itself, for example, controls when and when not the final -e should be pronounced. Chaucer cannot be 'translated' (or 'modernized'). There may be senses in which Latin, French, Italian, Greek or even Chinese may be 'translated' into English, but not Chaucer who simply *is* his own kind of English.

INTRODUCTION

I

Chaucer and Shakespeare

Dryden, trying to counteract what he evidently felt was an excessive contemporary respect for Latin and French, recognized Chaucer and Shakespeare—to a lesser degree Ben Jonson—as belonging in the *great* English tradition. His instinct was right. It is an association that needs continually to be borne in mind. The tendency to separate Chaucer from the rest of English literature, as a Middle English text, is always insidiously with us, especially among our academic teachers.

Chaucer's society is implied in Chaucer's poetry. We should not, of course, read Chaucer (or any author) merely to disocver what his society was like. The present value is in the poetry, not in the one-time society. Nevertheless, the complexity (and value) of that society is still, if it is anywhere, in the complexity (and value) of the poetry which is our present object. The rudiments and externals of what that society was like are, of course, known also from other sources; the social historians have constructed their own picture of it and have confirmed that in general it was a complex of little communities, each market-town being both the focus of local life and in touch with London. Chaucer's English, courtly as it is in one of its aspects, is rooted in the speech of what was still (allowing for expanding trades) a predominantly agricultural community.

The community that discovers itself in Chaucer is already recognizably the English community of Shakespeare. Mediaeval England did not dissolve suddenly and absolutely in the sixteenth century. Shakespeare and Ben

Jonson still belong to that older community. The habit of regarding these authors as the first of the moderns, rather than the last of the mediaevals, promotes the illusion of a radical division, rather than of an interplay, between themselves and their past. If they are moderns, Chaucer also is a modern; if Chaucer is mediaeval, they also are mediaeval. It is arguable (on the evidence of the unity in English literature since Chaucer) that there has been *one* complex English organic community from the thirteenth century,[1] that it attained a climax at the great Shakespearian moment, and that nearly everything of value in England—even in the twentieth century—has been its creation. If that is accurate, the early growing phase of English—the English language, consciousness and tradition[2]—was that to which Chaucer's poetry belongs. In this growing mediaeval phase English grew along with the other modern European languages and literatures; it grew first into Chaucer's English and then, at its supreme moment, into Shakespeare's. Shakespeare's English is the complex fulfilment of, or development from, Chaucer's.

The historians of the English language have never accounted for Chaucer's English. They quote John of Trevisa and remind us that French was still the language into which Latin had to be construed in the schools when Chaucer was a boy and that English was only allowed in the law courts after 1363. But schools and law courts are

[1] Of the very little English poetry *that has survived* from the thirteenth century *The Owl and the Nightingale* and a few lyrics are the first evidences of a mediaeval English community and a specifically English sensibility, and their significance is in relation to Chaucer's poetry. Further evidence is provided by the architecture (Early English), and the music, of the thirteenth century. Englishmen and a Scotsman (Grosseteste, Roger Bacon and Duns Scotus) belong to the history of European thought in the thirteenth century, but their Latin work can scarcely be taken as evidence of an English community and tradition.

[2] Our philological teachers do a great disservice in driving a wedge between what language is and what language means. Mediaeval English poems have too often been treated in university class-rooms and examination halls as collections of words in which certain vowel changes may be observed to have taken place.

conservative places.[1] It seems agreed that French was dying as a spoken language in England well before Chaucer's time—though Chaucer was almost certainly bilingual. The acquisition by English of a new vocabulary from French—expressing new concepts, a remarkable modification of consciousness—happened during the very phase when French was ceasing to be spoken. The impression that French was still the language of the Court in Chaucer's time has somehow become established. But English, the speech of the large body of the English folk in their village and market-town communities, *must* already before Chaucer's time have been the speech also of the gentlefolk as a whole in manor-house and monastery, castle and Court. The evidence of this is Chaucer's poetry itself. His English poetry implies the audience—the exceptionally cultivated audience—it was composed for. It is itself the evidence (as Professor Raleigh asserted so convincingly in *On Writers and Writing*)[2] that Chaucer must have heard much lively and witty conversation not—or not only—in French but in English.

'It is impossible to overpraise Chaucer's mastery of language. Here at the beginning, as it is commonly reckoned, of Modern English literature, is a treasury of perfect speech. We can trace his themes, and tell something of the events of his life. . . . But where did he get his style—from which it may be said that English literature has been (in some respects) a long falling away?

'What is the ordinary account? I do not wish to cite individual scholars, and there is no need. Take what can be gathered from the ordinary textbooks—what are the current ideas? Is not this a fair statement of them?

' "English was a despised language little used by the upper classes. A certain number of dreary works written chiefly for homiletic purposes or in order to appeal to the

---

[1] What is perhaps more significant is John of Trevisa's observation that, in his time, country gentlemen were no longer concerned that their sons should learn French in order to qualify as gentlemen.

[2] For permission to quote at length from this book I am indebted to the publishers, Edward Arnold & Co.

humble people, are to be found in the half-century before Chaucer. They are poor and flat and feeble, giving no promise of the new dawn. Then arose the morning star! Chaucer adopted the despised English tongue and set himself to modify it, to shape it, to polish it, to render it fit for his purpose. He imported words from the French; he purified the English of his time from its dross; he shaped it into a fit instrument for his use."

'Now I have no doubt that a competent philologist examining the facts could easily show that this account *must* be nonsense, from beginning to end. But even a literary critic can say something certain on the point—perhaps can even give aid by divination to the philologists, and tell them where it will best repay them to ply their pickaxes and spades.

'No poet makes his own language. No poet introduces serious or numerous modifications into the language that he uses. Some, no doubt, coin words and revive them, like Spenser or Keats in verse, Carlyle or Sir Thomas Browne in prose. But least of all great English poets did Chaucer mould and modify the speech he found. The poets who take liberties with speech are either prophets or eccentrics. From either of these characters Chaucer was far removed. He held fast by communal and social standards for literary speech. His English is plain, terse, homely, colloquial English, taken alive out of daily speech. He expresses his ideal again and again. . . .

'Chaucer has expressed his views on the model literary style so clearly and so often, and has illustrated them so well in his practice, that no mistake is possible. His style is the perfect courtly style; it has all the qualities of ease, directness, simplicity, of the best colloquial English, in short, which Chaucer recognized, three centuries before the French Academy, as the English spoken by cultivated women in society. His "facound", like Virginia's, "is ful womanly and pleyn". He avoids all "counterfeited terms", all subtleties of rhetoric, and addresses himself to the "commune intente".

'. . . Now a style like this, and in this perfection, implies a society at the back of it. If we are told that educated people at the Court of Edward III spoke French and that English was a despised tongue, we could deny it on the evidence of Chaucer alone. His language was not shaped by rustics. No English style draws so much as Chaucer's from the communal and colloquial elements of the language. And his poems make it certain that from his youth up he had heard much admirable witty talk in the English tongue.'

There could be no better start towards a criticism of Chaucer's poetry. Such a criticism may appropriately begin from a recognition that Chaucer's genius, like Shakespeare's, is rooted in the English language as it was spoken in his time. Chaucer's English is unmistakably the English of cultivated people; it is, as unmistakably, rooted in the speech of an agricultural folk. The great creative achievements of the Elizabethans are the work of men— Shakespeare, Marlowe, Ben Jonson, Donne—outside the Court.[1] Yet the completely English Chaucer was closely associated with his contemporary Court; and how otherwise then as completely English should the author of the *Canterbury Tales* be described?

The characteristics of a language—and therefore of a literature—are there from its beginning.[2] The characteristics of English literature—and of the English language —are revealed in Chaucer, the great fourteenth-century master of English. It is not enough merely to isolate here and there in Chaucer an un-Chaucerian line that might be from Spenser or Milton—

> Singest with vois memorial in the shade
> > (Anelida and Arcite)

or a line that might be from Donne—

[1] This is not to deny that Shakespeare and Ben Jonson were in touch with the Renaissance Court of Elizabeth and its adherents.

[2] The same appears to be true of music. The characteristics of French, English, German and Italian music are recognizable already in the thirteenth and fourteenth centuries.

I fond hir deed, and buried in an herte
(The Compleynte unto Pite).

It needs to be recognized that not only the poets but the great English dramatists and their successors, the novelists, form one unbroken development—the *great* development—from Chaucer; they are masters of the language of which Chaucer is, before them, the great master. We have too much neglected this essential unity of English literature within the larger unity of European literature.

The colloquial and highly dramatic character of the poetry of Chaucer and Shakespeare implies that, for both of them, poetry was a developed social art. Chaucer's poetry, though not like Shakespeare's intended for the theatre, reads as if it had been intended—as no doubt it was—to be read aloud to a company, the frequent dialogues being given full value. The Court itself must have been a more sophisticated kind of small town community and the talk there a cultivated version of small-town gossip; we seem, in listening to Chaucer's poetry, to hear that talk organized into a poetic art that is the nearest thing to dramatic art. The combination of easy familiarity and good breeding, of colloquialism and courtesy, evidences a harmonious social relationship between cultivated poet and cultivated audience. But that poet and that audience are, evidently, no more cut off than Shakespeare and the more cultivated part of *his* audience are from the vigorous life of the English people as a whole. Chaucer's poetry implies that his English community was, comparatively, a homogeneous community in which folk of diverse 'degrees' (the Knight and the Plowman) were interdependent and intimate, as by comparison persons in the modern classless mass are isolated; it implies, perhaps, the most nearly inclusive social order that has ever been implied in English and (despite the Peasants' Revolt) the most harmoniously integrated.[1] The scholarly and courtly

[1] R. J. Tiddy in his book *The Mummer's Play* stresses that, outside the villages, class distinctions were growing in importance in Chaucer's Eng-

20

Chaucer is a member of his whole contemporary English community; for the purposes of imaginative creation in language he had the same advantage as Shakespeare; his cultivated English is rooted in the speech—concrete, figurative, proverbial—of the agricultural English folk.

The colloquial vigour of the eighteenth-century English authors, who may be regarded as among Chaucer's successors, is by comparison with Chaucer's less in harmony with their celebrated 'politeness'. Both aspects of their mind and art have suffered a consequent coarsening—as Eliot has observed in comparing them with the authors of the early seventeenth century. Their 'politeness', by comparison with Chaucer's 'courteisye', is more a matter of formalized manners, stylized external deportment—'decorum'; Chaucer's 'courteisye' is a profounder and more spiritual quality; it proceeds, perhaps, from some English conjunction of the courtly tradition and mediaeval Christian tradition, as Dante's from a corresponding Italian conjunction. ('O anima cortese Mantovana')[1] The nearest that later English literature comes to Chaucer's 'courteisye' is in the courtesy of Shakespeare's noble and

land, but 'the very clearness with which distinctions were recognized seems to have made easier the interplay of class with class. However great may have been the political inequality of Chaucer's times the classes have never afterwards been so completely fused in social intercourse. . . . This alone must have tended to preserve an identity of taste in literature. . . . I doubt very much whether there was any great difference in the tastes of the different classes till the time of the Renaissance, when classical themes and elaborate psychology were introduced.'

[1] C. S. Lewis (in *The Allegory of Love*) has discussed at length the courtly love 'religion'—the 'religion' of Amor and of Venus—which borrows the mediaeval Christian terminology and is often a kind of reflection or solemn parody of the religion of Christ and Mary. Venus, in association with Nature, is frequently in mediaeval literature set in opposition to the Virgin as if in assertion of aspects of life which monastic Christianity attempted to reject. In Dante the courtly love of the troubadours is absorbed into the higher love; in Chaucer also one becomes aware of a harmony, as well as a distinction, between the lower and the higher spheres of love.

> . . . Madame, the god above
> Foryelde you, that ye the god of love
> Han maked me his wrathe to foryive.

courtly characters—in contrast to that atrocious French 'polish' of the 'fine gentlemen' of Restoration Comedy— and perhaps in George Herbert's poetry (as in the poem called *Love* in which God is the perfect considerate host, 'sweetly questioning if I lacked anything').

Chaucer's 'tolerance'—which should rather be called 'charity' or 'benignity'—should also be distinguished from eighteenth-century 'tolerance'. The latter, 'rational' as it was, and, in the aspect of 'toleration', serving as a useful expedient to promote social and political compromise and comfort, was apt to degenerate into moral complacency. The difference between Chaucer and the eighteenth century in general is the difference between a mind which distinguishes the subtleties of evil from the delicacies of good and one for which such distinctions (though still made) have become blunter. The *great* authors, who are also the great moralists, of the eighteenth century—Pope, Samuel Johnson, Crabbe, Jane Austen—seem, therefore, less at ease in their society than Chaucer seems in his.

We must take account, of course, of Arnold's charge that Chaucer's poetry lacks 'high seriousness' such as that of Dante. The answer surely is that Chaucer's mature poetry of the human comedy has behind it the weight and gravity of his whole mediaeval civilization, English and European, religious and humane. Chaucer is rational with that high mediaeval rationality and should in this respect also be associated with Shakespeare. Eliot and Santayana have both, differently, made the point that whereas Dante's poetry has behind it the philosophy of Aquinas, Shakespeare has only a version of Seneca, the Roman moralist and tragedian whom the Renaissance so astonishingly elevated; and that Shakespeare's philosophy may be summed up as 'Duncan is in his grave'. Santayana quotes Macbeth's 'To-morrow and to-morrow and to-morrow . . .' speech as if it summed up Shakespeare's view of life. That dramatic speech expresses, not the dramatist's view of life, but the *dramatis persona's*, at the tragic conclusion of his career; Shakespeare's meaning is the meaning of the *whole* play.[1] The divinely established natural order which Macbeth disturbs by his 'unnatural' act is concretely *there*—directly present to the senses—in the poetry of the scene in which the good king, Duncan, approaches Macbeth's castle,[2] and elsewhere in the texture of the whole play. There, even in Shakespeare's darkest play, is Shakespeare's 'belief'. His conception of man and the universe (which contends against his acute consciousness of disorder) is essentially that which is expressed in the opening passage of the *Canterbury Tales*. This is borne out in each one of the plays—in none more wonderfully perhaps than in *A Winter Tale*—for Shakespeare's total meaning (as Eliot has said) is not even the meaning of a whole play but of *all* the plays in the order which they establish among themselves.

The rationality which Chaucer shares with Shakespeare and Dante is rooted in his perhaps more undisturbed membership of his whole agricultural community in harmony with the rhythms of nature. The gaiety, and at times jollity, of his poetry suggests an association between it and the spring seasonal festivals of both village and courtly folk; it has its roots in the earth and unfolds into a larger and deeper humane graciousness whose shadowed depth is the mediaeval rational gravity. Chaucer's sustained rational joyousness includes profound charitableness and clear critical vision; it is less intense than the joy of the *Paradiso* (the joy that begins to be felt already in the *Purgatorio* when Matilda approaches in the garden of the Earthly Paradise); it is less profoundly mystical than the joyous apprehension of an ultimate harmony, even in proximity to acute consciousness of the disharmony of evil, in *A Winter's Tale*, *The Tempest* and *Pericles*; Chaucer's human

[1] The reader may be referred to *Tragedy and the Medium: A Note on Mr. Santayana's Tragic Philosophy* by F. R. Leavis. (See *The Common Pursuit*.)

[2] Mr. Leavis and Mr. L. C. Knights have shown this in their analyses in, respectively, *Education and the University* and *Explorations*.

comedy of Pandarus, the Wife of Bath or Chauntecleer is nearer to that of Falstaff or Mistress Quickly than to the sphere of Prospero or Marina. Yet Chaucer's robust and racy Englishness is reconciled with his mediaeval courtesy and Christian charity. Perhaps because he is less disturbed by life than Dante or Shakespeare he never attains their 'ultimate vision'; but his joy has its roots in that rational and humane Christian civilization which he shares with both.

In a century such as our own it is fatally easy to look back to the past with nostalgia instead of bringing the past to bear on the understanding and criticism of the present. We must beware therefore of idealizing the world which was the object of Chaucer's contemplation; Chaucer himself does *not* idealize it and, therefore, if we read Chaucer rightly we shall not do so either. In the world of Chaucer's contemplation characters are presented and identified, each according to its kind, with a concrete distinctness and a moral clarity that corresponds to the art which sharply distinguishes particular characters in the *Inferno*. The civilization is in the quality of the contemplation, not in the objects contemplated. Chaucer contemplates them with a serene humanity that not only identifies but *accepts* each in its different kind, both good and evil, as making up the sum of living creatures—'God's plenty'—planted in that which is beyond Good and Evil, being the Perfection of their Creator. An impression of 'God's plenty' keeps recurring to the English imagination—the 'various light' of Marvell's *Garden*, the 'dapple' (the 'veined, stained, skeined variety') in Gerard Manley Hopkins's poetry, and in Yeats's *Sailing to Byzantium*

> . . . birds in the trees,
> —Those dying generations—at their song,
> The salmon-falls, the mackerel-crowded seas,
> Fish, flesh, or fowl . . .

But when the variety and dramatic energy and the completeness of Chaucer's human comedy are considered, the

claim that Chaucer is not only the first great English auth-
or but the greatest next only to Shakespeare may well
seem the inevitable one.

2

Simile and Allegory

Once the community (in both senses) between Chaucer
and Shakespeare has been recognized it is possible to
qualify that recognition by making the distinctions. What
may (for example) at first disconcert the reader coming to
the poetry of Chaucer from the poetry of the complex
Shakespearian phase of English civilization is that there
are not the ambiguities and involvements of phrase and
rhythm there are in Shakespeare, Ben Jonson, the other
mature Elizabethan dramatists, Donne, Herbert and Marvell. Chaucer's phrases have an immediacy and vividness
of image unmatched outside Shakespeare. Yet Chaucer's
phrases appear almost disconcertingly simple and direct
to a reader accustomed to the complexities, the encrusta-
tions of meaning involved in Shakespearian metaphor.
Shakespeare's metaphors take effect instantaneously, but
there is characteristically a remarkable complexity of meaning involved in them. Similes, not metaphors, are what are
characteristic of Chaucer (as of Dante, as Eliot has noted),
and they promote lucidly the visualization essential to
allegorical vision. For Chaucer's poetry may be understood as growing out of allegory. It grows well beyond
allegory in the human comedy of *Troilus and Criseyde* and
the *Canterbury Tales*. Nevertheless, we will not understand
the art and vision of the Chaucerian poetry of the human
comedy unless we understand that it has developed without any absolute break from allegory. It would be easy to
be deceived into supposing that no profundities of meaning comparable to the Shakespearian are concealed within
the crystal transparency of the Chaucerian phrases. If (as

25

Mr. Wilson Knight has said) a Shakespeare play may be regarded as an 'expanded metaphor', a mediaeval allegorical poem may perhaps be regarded as an 'expanded simile'. An 'expanded simile' better describes the simpler lucidity of the allegorical structure. The difference may perhaps serve to suggest the difference between the Shakespearian and the Chaucerian structures. Even the great poems of Chaucer which have grown well beyond allegory have grown from allegory and reveal their original structures under analysis.

The account of Chaucer according to which he progressed from allegory to realism is therefore a simplification which may be misleading. Chaucer's most 'realistic' poems—the poems in which he presents the human comedy as a directly observed thing—have not severed their connection with their origins in allegory, but are rather extensions from allegory on to the plane of his direct—or less directed—observation of life. Realism is not at all incompatible with allegory as we are apt to imagine. Mediaeval visions, *Piers Plowman* for example, are often more sharply 'realistic' in some of their scenes than modern novels. Allegory and personification provided Chaucer's observation with an initial guiding method and his judgment with an initial scale of values which his observation gradually clarified and which clarified his observation. Underneath Chaucer's presentation (almost dramatization) of the human comedy remain the mediaeval allegorical and moral patterns. The poems gain in profundity and variety from the mutual enrichment of these multiplex layers of meaning, though the Chaucerian phrase in itself is to the end remarkable for its crystalline and limpid simplicity. Chaucer has the faculty of seeming more simple than he is.

Chaucer may at first appear subdued—prosaic almost —by comparison with the hyperbolical pride of Elizabethan rhetoric. There is no exaggeration in Chaucerian art, which corresponds in this respect to his mediaeval humility. For behind the simplicity and naturalness which so delighted Coleridge and Wordsworth in Chaucer there is art laboriously and slowly perfected with deliberate, disciplined 'devocioun'—

> The lyf so short, the craft so long to lerne.

Chaucer's is a profoundly civilized simplicity and should not be mistaken for a primitive unsophisticated naïveté, however charming. Beside that Chaucerian simplicity the early Elizabethan pompous magnificence looks almost barbaric. Professor Manly in his pamphlet, *Chaucer and the Rhetoricians*, indicates how thoroughly grounded Chaucer was in the scholastic 'rhetoric', which he was sufficiently skilled in, as well as conscious of, to parody in the *Nun's Priest's Tale* and elsewhere. This 'rhetoric'—often a series of *exempla*—leaves the simplicity and directness of Chaucerian phrase intact. There is no resemblance between it and, for example, the 'rhetoric' of early Elizabethan dramatic poetry. Here we are using 'rhetoric' in two quite different senses. Mediaeval 'rhetoric', the particular conception of the art of literary expression carefully formulated by the schools, appears neither to have impeded nor modified Chaucer's colloquial strength.

3

Borrowing and Originality

The bibliography and references to sources which Chaucer might be said—from a modern viewpoint—to have omitted to append to his work would have been most extensive, and as distracting in effect, perhaps, as the notes to the *Waste Land* proved. The detective work which this omission has provoked discloses whole passages of Chaucer's poetry as lifted from one or another French, Italian or Latin 'source', and that borrowings from diverse sources adjoin each other or are combined. Yet the work of any poet might by similar methods be exposed as a complex of conscious or unconscious borrowings. Chaucer's borrowings have the advantage of being conscious and deliberate; he knew all the time, as Shakespeare did in handling *his* sources, completely what he was doing; we need be concerned only with what he has done. For this diversity of literary source is invariably quite unfelt in the result which could not be mistaken for the French poetry of Guillaume de Lorris or Jean de Meung, Machaut, Froissart or Deschamps; the Italian poetry of Boccaccio, Petrarch or Dante; the Latin poetry of Ovid. Chaucer's poetry has its own English uniqueness.

It is this unique Chaucerian character which is the object of criticism, from the apprehension of which it ought not to be distracted. If Chaucer is unique, and greater than his literary originals (Dante perhaps excepted), the uniqueness and greatness evidently inhere in that Chaucerian character which the elucidation of literary sources may as easily obscure as—judiciously used—focus. The investigation line by line of literary sources points beyond the limits not only of what is readily practicable but of what is relevant to criticism, which is concerned with seeing what *is*, however it arrived at being so; and that, in Chaucer's case, is distinct from any of his literary sources, or from any combination of them; it is the poetry of Chaucer, which is there as something to be as far as possible directly and accurately apprehended.

The emphasis has, indeed, been placed differently by different scholars as to Chaucer's relative indebtedness to his different French, Italian, Latin sources. If we think only of literary sources it is, however, sufficiently evident that he begins (in his poetry as we have it) from *both* parts of the *Roman de la Rose* which remain his principal French sources whatever may be his indebtedness also to his French contemporaries. His most substantial Italian sources —and they are very substantial—are *Il Filostrato* and *Teseide* (but not, apparently, the *Decameron*) of Boccaccio. Of the Roman poets it appears, from a comparison, likely that he had the Latin of Ovid frequently before him and did not depend on the French mediaevalizations of that poet. The most celebrated stories of Graeco-Roman antiquity were certainly available to him also in their French mediaevalizations. We have, of course, to take account not only of what was read by Chaucer but how it was read; the mediaeval mind of Chaucer mediaevalizes even its direct impressions of Virgil and Ovid. Chaucer was, besides, as 'learned' a poet in his world as any seventeenth-century poet in his—well acquainted with the philosophy and science (astronomy, alchemy, physics, medicine) of his learned mediaeval Latin world. Nor need what happens to be known of his biography be invoked to testify, as it so conveniently does, to Chaucer's exceptional first-hand acquaintance with his contemporary English and European world of diverse people and affairs; his poetry is again the direct evidence.

Chaucer (it might be claimed) is the first Englishman who is great both as an Englishman and a European. It may be doubted whether an Englishman can be in any complete sense an Englishman who is not in the same sense a European; the one is implied in the other (the equivalent might be argued of a Frenchman, a German, an Italian—or an American). Chaucer, as the development of his poetry shows, became consciously an English poet —consciously a master of English—through his work of translating, paraphrasing and adapting from other European languages (French, Italian and Latin) and thus assimilating essential European tradition. He became consciously an Englishman, as distinct from a Frenchman or Italian, as he became conscious of the powers—particularly the dramatic power—of his English language as distinct from the powers of French, Latin, Italian.

It is doubtful whether any later English author has been both more English than Chaucer and closer to the essentials of French, Latin and Italian, not excepting Ben Jonson or Andrew Marvell. It is frequently repeated that Shakespeare was no scholar. But if Shakespeare is not centrally in the European tradition who (it may be asked) is? Shakespeare is a more conscious and a greater European, as he is a more conscious and a greater Englishman, than any of his contemporary 'scholars' and in this respect certainly nearer Chaucer than they. Milton's scholarship, though it meant so much to him personally, is a remoter because more independent thing, and Milton, though a great Englishman, is more limited an Englishman than Shakespeare or Chaucer. Eighteenth-century 'classical education' is already very formal, though not yet entirely the formality it later became.

The emergence of an English poet of the European greatness of Chaucer by the end of the fourteenth century (a fully English creative moment, which yielded simultaneously also *Piers Plowman* and *Sir Gawayn and the Grene Knight* and, probably, many of the best Carols and Miracle Plays) *implies* a vivid English community and a vivid English language. It must necessarily have involved (the editors and scholars have sufficiently demonstrated that it did) an enormous technical and imaginative effort, a labour of assimilation, adaptation and re-creation of French, Latin and Italian modes and themes that would have been beyond the scope of any but a poet of quite remarkable *English* genius; Chaucer in fact possessed resources of his own, English resources, which he discovered how to use and develop.

For Chaucer's sources were not merely literary sources. His fundamental source was his English language itself. The vitality and vividness of Chaucer's human comedy springs from that common source, that 'well of English', which later was Shakespeare's also. The characters of that human comedy are already recognizably English men and women, members of a community with the characters of later English literature; Pandarus and Criseyde, the Prioress, the Monk, and the Friar (and that other Friar of the *Somnour's Tale*), the Pardoner, the Wife of Bath, Alisoun and Absolon, Januarie and May, Chauntecleer and Pertelote—there are in later English literature no characters *more* vivid than these, whether as they are initially presented, or as they move and talk in scenes and dialogues that are surely the nearest thing in English to sheer drama outside the Shakespearian drama itself. The dialogues in particular have the immediacy of dialogues that are actually listened to and the scenes the immediacy of scenes actually witnessed. English as Chaucer uses it already shows that particular dramatic power which it characteristically shows at its creative moments not only in poetry but also in plays and novels. That vividness is controlled in Chaucer's poetry by an art which implies a delicate and sure criticism of life. No literary historian can adequately account for that art. There is nothing in what we know of the literature and society of the time that can adequately do so. There is no clearer case of original genius. Arnold salutes the fact in his paragraphs on Chaucer in *The Study of Poetry* which are our finest, our sanest criticism of Chaucer. Civilization in any age has reached its highest point only in an exceptional individual.

PART ONE

TO THE CANTERBURY TALES

THE EARLIER POEMS

*The Romaunt of the Rose, The Boke of the Duchesse,
The Hous of Fame, The Parlement of Foules*

Regarded as nearly as possible in the order in which they
were composed the poems of Chaucer, like the plays of
Shakespeare, are seen to form a pattern which is the pattern of a continuous process of growth. In that process
each successive poem marks a stage. Chaucer's poetry as
a whole may be understood as that process of growth which
culminates in the *Canterbury Tales*.

I

THE ROMAUNT OF THE ROSE

Chaucer begins (in his extant work) as a translator of the
Roman de la Rose. For it is not in dispute that he translated
the poem (or part of it) and who else could have composed
the first part at least of the Chaucerian *Romaunt of the Rose*?
In any case the French poem remains Chaucer's primary
literary source—or sources; there are in the poem two
diverse sources, Guillaume de Lorris's original allegory
and Jean de Meung's continuation which is not at all a
continuation of Guillaume. In the end it is Jean de Meung
who appears the more congenial of the two to Chaucer—
Jean de Meung who associates easily with the *fabliaux*.
C. S. Lewis in the *Allegory of Love* would describe even
Troilus and Criseyde in terms of Guillaume's allegory. But
Troilus and Criseyde cannot, any more than can the *Canter-*

bury Tales themselves, be accounted for by this or by any other of the literary sources; they can only be accounted for by giving the fullest credit to the creativeness of Chaucer's English—in effect to Chaucer's English genius.

The new music is, of course, what first enchants those who attend to the Chaucerian *Romaunt of the Rose*, the new music, heard for the first time sustainedly in English, of the mediaeval lyric poetry of youthful delight associated with the spring festivals and the courtly 'carol'.

> Tho mightest thou caroles seen,
> And folk ther daunce and mery been,
> And make many a fair tourning
> Upon the grene gras springing.
> Ther mightest thou see these floutours,
> Minstrales, and eek jogelours,
> That wel to singe dide hir peyne.
> Somme songe songes of Loreyne;
> For in Loreyne hir notes be
> Ful swetter than in this contree.
>
> .   .   .   .   .
>
> A lady gan me for to espye,
> And she was cleped Curtesye,
> The worshipful, the debonaire;
> I pray god ever falle hir faire!
> Ful curteisly she called me,
> 'What do ye there, beau sire?' quod she,
> 'Come neer, and if it lyke yow
> To dauncen, daunceth with us now.'
> And I, withoute tarying,
> Wente into the caroling.

But what concerns me here, with ultimately the *Canterbury Tales* in view, is to notice that the elements of Chaucer's mature art are present from the beginning, and may be observed in their primary form in the *Romaunt of the Rose*. The process of growth of Chaucer's art is the process by which the personifications of the *Romaunt of the Rose* grow

36

into the persons of the *Canterbury Tales*. The conventional figures and types first exhibited in the *Romaunt of the Rose* are more and more particularized, and thus individualized, in each successive poem as Chaucer's personal observation and growing experience of the actual world of humans successively re-creates them. The personification, Ydelnesse, includes elements and features which are incorporated in the appearance of the Prioresse (though the Prioresse is as a whole nearer Curtesye).

> Hir nose of good proporcioun,
> Hir yen greye as a faucoun . . .
> With litel mouth, and round to see;
> A clove chin eek hadde she.

But Ydelnesse is a generalization that many diverse Chaucerian ladies besides the Prioresse, may be related back to. Sir Mirthe is in the same way the generalized basis not only of the young Squire but of all the young bachelors— and many of the young women as well—of the *Canterbury Tales*.

> As round as appel was his face,
> Ful rody and whyt in every place.
> Fetys he was and wel beseye,
> With metely mouth and yen greye;
> His nose by mesure wrought ful right;
> Crisp was his heer, and eek ful bright.

The visualization of these figures of an allegorical vision is clearly of primary importance, and remains important in the presentation of 'character' later in the Chaucerian human comedy. Similes, some of them already 'taken alive out of English daily speech', are what principally promote, as much more freely in the *Canterbury Tales*, the clear visualization.

> As round as appel was his face . . .

> Hir heer was as yelowe of hewe
> As any basin scoured newe . . .

37

There is nothing in the French corresponding to 'round', which introduces a tactual value giving solidity to the image; nor is there anything in the French corresponding to that 'scoured newe' which brings the second simile to life.

Jean de Meung's continuation provided Chaucer with the more vigorous root of the two. That encyclopaedic composition provided Chaucer with a great deal of sheer substance. In it are found the important personifications, Nature and Reason (philosophic concepts which, like Fortune, had taken on a life more real than the faded Olympians except Venus and were now involved with the Christian hierarchy); and in it are debates, such as those on dreams and predestination, which Chaucer continued even in the *Canterbury Tales* to develop. All this substance goes back, of course, to earlier 'authorities' such as Boethius, and these Chaucer certainly resorted to directly. But Jean de Meung had conveniently brought it together; and Jean contributes a sceptical tone and attitude.[1] That sceptical tone and attitude—similar to the tone and attitude of the *fabliaux*—was certainly more congenial to Chaucer's development as a poet of the human comedy than the courtly tone and attitude of Guillaume.

To look more particularly at this part. Once again we find elementary originals of some of the characters of the *Canterbury Tales*.[2] In Fals-Semblant are rudimentarily present the ecclesiastics, the monks and friars who enliven and bulk so large in the human comedy of the *Canterbury Tales*.

> Amour. 'Thou prechest abstinence also?'
> F.Sem. 'Sir, I wol fillen, so mote I go,
> My paunche of gode mete and wyne,
> As shulde a maister of divyne;
> For how that I me pover feyne,

[1] The French sceptical tradition began before Montaigne.

[2] Some of the rudiments of the Wife of Bath may be just discerned in the Vekke (Old Woman) who appears in both parts—'For she knew al the olde dance.'

> Yit alle pore folk I disdeyne.
>   'I love bet the acqueyntaunce
> Ten tymes, of the king of Fraunce,
> Than of pore man of mylde mode,
> Though that his soule be also gode . . .
> Let bere hem to the spitel anoon,
> But, for me, comfort gete they noon.
> But a riche sike usurere
> Wolde I visyte and drawe nere;
> Him wol I comforte and rehete,
> For I hope of his gold to gete . . .
> I rekke not of pore men,
> Hir astate is not worth an hen.
> Where findest thou a swinker of labour
> Have me unto his confessour?

Features of the Friar and the Monk of the great Prologue are discernible in several of the phrases. The more vigorous realism of Jean de Meung, his introduction of the world as he sharply observed it into the allegory, is developed still further by the translation of it into English phrases with a vigour of their own.

> But Beggers with these hodes wyde,
> With sleighe and pale faces lene,
> And greye clothes not ful clene.

The realistic phantasmagoria includes those fine speciments of the Seven Deadly Sins, Coveityse and Glotonye. When Fals-Semblant speaks of 'fyn vitaille',

> That we, under our clothes wyde
> Maken thurgh our golet glyde,

he uses a phrase that burgeons again in the Pardoner's sermon on 'glotonye' embodied in his tale.

The disenchanting spirit present in Jean de Meung continues to be an element in Chaucer's maturer and completer intelligence. The presence of this sceptical common-sense forces a revision of the values of Guillaume's allegory, subjecting love, courtly love ('It is a syknesse of the thought'), to the criticism of Raisoun.

> For to gete and have the Rose
> Which maketh thee so mate and wood
> That thou desirest noon other good.

No 'good' other than 'to gete and have the Rose' had been proposed in the first part of the poem, even allowing that the Rose means something rather different in the two parts. There is thus in the second part a shift of values resulting not only from a sceptical attitude to love but from a realization that there are other values. Towards these other values, which are related to the values of Religion, Raisoun directs.

In the poems of Chaucer that immediately succeed the *Romaunt of the Rose*[1] the allegorical designs remain—these poems are again dreams or visions—but what we may observe is a deepening humanization of the designs and a developing dramatic genius.

2

THE BOKE OF THE DUCHESSE

The *Boke of the Duchesse* is an unmistakable offshoot of the first part of the *Roman de la Rose*, and an early exercise. The version of Ovid's Ceyx and Alcyone that forms its Prologue may be earlier still, and is notable only for a Spenserian line or two describing the Cave of Sleep where a stream

> Came renning fro the cliffes adoun,
> That made a deedly sleping soun,

[1] Whether or not Fragments B and C are Chaucer's need not alter our estimate of the effect of the *Roman de la Rose* on Chaucer's work. No other English translator of the *Roman de la Rose* is in fact known. The northern forms of Fragment B are explainable if it is a copy of Chaucer's version modified by having been made (let us say) in Lincolnshire.

> And ronnen doun right by a cave
> That was under a rokke y-grave[1]

and a dramatic moment when the ghost of Alcyone's drowned husband stands by her bedside; it is this latter element which is to develop in Chaucer's poetry.

But to turn from the Prologue to the dream or vision itself. The confrontation of the dreamer by the man in black has both a dramatic and an allegorical character. The deep allegorizing, personifying impulse of the mediaeval mind persists in the idiom itself. When the mourner exclaims

> Allas, o deeth! what ayleth thee,
> That thou noldest have taken me,
> Whan that thou toke my lady swete?
> That was so fayr, so fresh, so free . . .

death is a person—and is a person still in the idiom of the *Canterbury Tales*. The man in black himself readily slips back—or is extended—into identification with Sorrow.

> For I am sorwe and sorwe is I.

But it is in the occasional dramatic unexpectedness and the momentary revelations of profound humanity that we become aware, even in the too diffuse *Boke of the Duchesse*, of the developing Chaucer—in the profound tenderness of

> . . . for be it never so derke
> Me thinketh I see hir ever mo

and in the presentation, dramatization almost, of the young girl, Blanche. For though the poem is an elegy, it is the living girl, Blanche, whose image—very characteristically

---

[1] Chaucer evidently could have been Spenser if he had not cared to be something more interesting; this passage culminates in the most un-Spenserian and humorously dramatic—

> 'Awak!' quod he, 'who is lyth there?'
> And blew his horn right in hir ere.

of Chaucer—we remember from the poem, the first in the succession of vivid Chaucerian women.

> I saw hir daunce so comlily,
> Carole and singe so swetely,
> Laughe and pleye so womanly,
> And loke so debonairly.

Froissart describes the historical Blanche, the young Duchess, the beauty of the court of Edward III. 'She died young and *jolie*, about 22 years old, gay, gladsome, fresh, merry, sweet, simple, of modest bearing, the good lady whose name was Blanche.' In Chaucer she is *seen*—'Me thinketh I see hir ever mo'—'I saw hir daunce . . .'. We are presented with the impression of her immediate joyous presence—against the darkness of her absence.

3

THE HOUS OF FAME

The Hous of Fame is again in the short octosyllabic line of the *Romaunt of the Rose* and the *Boke of the Duchesse*. Yet there has been such an inflow of fresh conceptions from Dante and Ovid and other sources that it is masterly how they have been absorbed into a growing maturity, how we are not left with any irksome feeling of a form too slight and light not to break under such an abundance and expansion. The poem is in this respect preserved, perhaps, by its very diffusion. It remains perfectly conversational and easy. Chaucer's poems were evidently composed for a leisurely, as well as leisured, gossiping society; and the tone is often pleasantly intimate and humorous. *The Hous of Fame* is almost garrulous. But the garrulity here accords with the poet's humorous self-dramatization; and the dramatized clerkly Eagle (predecessor of Chauntecleer) is correspondingly a garrulous bird. This informal poem must not be read solemnly. The way the comparison with

Dante is sometimes made is misleading as well as damaging. There is a correspondence in the design and in the detail—in the actual handling of words by the two mediaeval poets. Chaucer's similes correspond to Dante's in being used to clarify and animate rather than decorate.

> But as a blinde man stert a hare . . .

> . . . . and ful eek of windowes
> As flakes falle in grete snowes . . .

> The halle was al ful y-wis
> Of hem that writen olde gestes
> As ben on trees rokkes nestes . . .

> As men a pot-ful bawme helde
> Among a basket ful of roses . . .

But in the *Hous of Fame* this design and method which Chaucer shares with Dante—and may here have partly adapted from Dante—is working towards a different end. That end is high comedy. For whatever may have been said about it being a failure to scale the Dantean sublime (inexcusably confused with the Miltonic sublime) Chaucer's poem is quite unpretentious in tone and belongs to the realm of the phantastic serio-comic. Allegory need not be solemn, and comedy here relates to allegory.

The second and third books need alone concern us. The miniature of the *Aeneid* in the first book (The Prologue) looks like earlier work. The maturer poem begins at the very end of the first book and the beginning of the second when the poet finds himself unexpectedly the most recent in the long succession of ascents. Borne upwards in the eagle's talons he wonders 'wher Jove wol me stellifye'. This tone of burlesque is the tone of the prolonged colloquy in the second book between the clerkly eagle and the bewildered poet in his bizarre situation in the eagle's talons.

But to see more clearly the significance of the poem it may be expedient to turn first to the third book where the comedy becomes more gravely ironic and responsible.

> 'But what art thou that seyst this tale,
> That werest on thy hose a pale,
> And on thy tipet swiche a belle!'
> 'Madame,' quod he, 'sooth to telle,
> I am that ilke shrewe, y-wis,
> That brende the temple of Isidis
> In Athenes, lo, that citee.'
> 'And wherfor didest thou so?' quod she.
> 'By my thrift,' quod he, 'madame,
> I wolde fayn han had a fame,
> As other folk hadde in the toun,
> Al-thogh they were of greet renoun
> For hir vertu and for hir thewes;
> Thoughte I, as greet a fame han shrewes,
> Thogh hit be but for shrewednesse,
> As gode folk han for goodnesse;
> And sith I may not have that oon,
> That other nil I noght for-goon.
> And for to gette of Fames hyre,
> The temple sett I al a-fyre.

There the allegory and the comedy—the imaginative vision and the ironic contemplation of original folly—are one. Pope's *Dunciad* is the baroque successor of Chaucer's *Hous of Fame*. Fame, one of the primary objects of human ambition, is no more substantial than air, mere conflicting wind and noise, vanity.

> 'Maistow not heren that I do?'
> 'What?' quod I. 'The grete soun',
> Quod he, 'that rumbleth up and doun
> In Fames Hous, ful of tydinges,
> Bothe of fair speche and chydinges,
> And of fals and soth compouned . . .
> Nay, dred thee not thereof', quod he,
> 'Hit is nothing wil byten thee;
> Thou shalt non harm have, trewely.'

44

The phantastic, as in the description of a true and a false rumour meeting, is therefore itself an element in the ironic comedy.

> And somtyme saugh I tho, at ones,
> A lesing and a sad soth-sawe,
> That gonne of aventure drawe
> Out at a windowe for to pace;
> And, when they metten in that place,
> They were a-chekked bothe two,
> And neither of hem moste out go;
> For other so they gonne croude,
> Til eche of hem gan cryen loude,
> 'Lat me go first!' 'Nay, but lat me!
> And here I wol ensuren thee
> With the nones that thou wolt do so,
> That I shal never fro thee go,
> But be thyn owne sworen brother!
> We will medle us ech with other,
> That no man, be he never so wrothe,
> Shal han that oon of two, but bothe
> At ones, al beside his leve,
> Come we a-morwe or on eve,
> Be we cryed or stille y-rouned.'
> Thus saugh I fals and soothe compouned
> Togeder flee for oo tydinge.

To return to the second book. We see now how beautifully it burlesques the absurdity of pedantry which Chaucer, himself so learned, seems aware he risked. The pedantic bird in mid-air, for the benefit of the uncomfortably situated but still curious poet, launches on a scientific exposition, an explication of how sounds travel to Fame's house.

> 'Soun is noght but air y-broken,
> And every speche that is spoken,
> Loud or privee, foul or fair,
> In his substaunce is but air;
> For as flaumbe is but lighted smoke,

45

Right so soun is air y-broke.
But this may be in many wyse,
Of which I will thee two devyse,
As soun that comth of pype or harpe.
For whan a pype is blowen sharpe,
The air is twist with violence,
And rent; lo, this is my sentence;
Eek, whan men harpe-stringes smyte,
Whether hit be moche or lyte,
Lo, with the strook the air to-breketh;
Right so hit breketh whan men speketh.
Thus wost thou wel what thing is speche.
Now hennesforth I wol thee teche,
How every speche, or noise, or soun,
Through his multiplicacioun,
Thogh hit were pyped of a mous,
Moot nede come to Fames Hous.
I preve hit thus—tak hede now—
By experience; for if that thou
Throwe on water now a stoon,
Wel wost thou, hit wol make anoon
A litel roundel as a cercle,
Paraunture brood as a covercle;
And right anoon thou shalt see weel,
That wheel wol cause another wheel,
And that the thridde, and so forth, brother,
Every cercle causing other, . . .
And right thus every word, y-wis,
That loude or privee spoken is,
Moveth first an air aboute,
And of this moving, out of doute,
Another air anoon is meved,
As I have of the water preved,
That every cercle causeth other.
Right so of air, my leve brother;
Everich air in other stereth
More and more, and speche up bereth,
Or vois, or noise, or word, or soun,

> Ay through multiplicacioun,
> Til hit be atte Hous of Fame;—
> Tak hit in ernest or in game.

How seriously we need take it the final dismissal—'tak hit in ernest or in game'—indicates. Besides being excellent parody—it sounds like a lecture by a modern scientific professor, intellectual pomposity and pedantic portentousness conveyed in the rhythm—it enforces the recognition of vanity, the awareness of emptiness which sustains the whole grand ironic comedy. The high wisdom of the mediaeval poet, hostile to all forms of illusion and delusion, is seen dissolving the clouds.

> 'O Crist', thoughte I, 'that art in blisse,
> Fro fantom and illusioun
> Me save!' and with devocioun
> Myn yën to the heven I caste.

(These lines come already at the end of the first book.) Chaucer's rational intelligence and his religious feeling are in no way antagonistic.

4

THE PARLEMENT OF FOULES

The Parlement of Foules has a limited, rounded completeness that the *Hous of Fame* lacks. It does what it sets out to do completely, but then it does not set out to do so much as the *Hous of Fame*. The 'political' allegory seems unimportant. The poem can be enjoyed as much even if we have forgotten which proposed royal betrothal (probably that of Anne of Bohemia and Richard II) it may have been intended to refer to. What matters is that it is a St. Valentine's Day poem, a joyous celebration of the early spring festival day on which the birds choose their mates for the year. There are certain stanzas (the poem is not accidentally in stanzas) describing the pageantry in the garden in which we become suddenly conscious of early Renaissance Italy. (These stanzas turn out to be a rendering of certain stanzas of Boccaccio.) But the garden of this particular vision has principally the character of the garden of Kynd as is appropriate to the St. Valentine's Day theme; in this garden the birds congregate to choose their mates.

It is in the dialogues of the bird 'debate' that the *Parlement of Foules* attains a maximum, a plenitude of dramatic English life. In Chaucer's acknowledged literary authority here (the *De Planctu Naturae* of Alanus de Insulis) the birds are mere pattern on Nature's dress. The real source of the birds in Chaucer's poem is the popular bird and beast fables. In the comedy of the clashes (the 'flytings') among the birds, between the 'cherls' and 'gentils', both sides share the same colloquial English idiom. The dialogue has the suppleness of life; the speaking voice is in full possession of the accomplished verse.

> 'Lo here! a parfit reson of a goos!'
> Quod the sperhauk; 'never mot she thee!
> Lo, swich hit is to have a tonge loos' . . .

> 'Now fy, cherl!' quod the gentil tercelet,
> 'Out of the dunghil com that word ful right,
> Thou canst noght see which thing is wel be-set:
> Thou farest by love as oules doon by light . . .

> 'Ye! have the glotoun fild ynogh his paunche,
> Then are we wel!' seyde the merlioun;
> 'Thou mordrer of the heysugge on the braunche . . .

The birds are a promise of Chaucer's Canterbury pilgrims; they are a company of English folk talking and disputing.

TROILUS AND CRISEYDE

I

In *Troilus and Criseyde* Chaucer is revealed as the great mediaeval master of the human comedy—a supremacy finally established by the *Canterbury Tales*. Pandarus is the first rounded comic creation of substantial magnitude in English literature; his successor is Falstaff (as Sir Epicure Mammon, on the other hand, comes in the succession from the Seven Deadly Sins). Criseyde is the first completely realized woman in English literature. But it is not as detached persons that Pandarus and Criseyde exist but as *personae* that speak and act in the drama (or novel) of the poem. The poem is, of course, as it concludes, the tragedy of Troilus—and Criseyde. But the tragedy depends for effectiveness on the actuality of the succession of dramatic scenes of the human comedy from which it evolves. The poem develops an actuality of comedy, radically beyond the sphere of courtly romance, and can accordingly move towards the complementary actuality of tragedy.

Troilus and Criseyde has been called a novel in verse.[1] Chaucer is here, as in the *Canterbury Tales*, poet, dramatist, novelist in one. It is sufficiently exact to say that Chaucer is here doing with words in verse the kind of thing that a great novelist, James or Conrad or Tolstoy, is doing with words in prose. We find the same delicacy of precision in the creative use of words, the same subtle responsiveness to changes and varieties of tone and attitude in the presentation of characters and scenes. The scenes of the Chaucerian human comedy have a vividness

[1] What, after all, is a *novel* but another kind of poem? The distinctions made between what is a poem, a play and a novel are apt only to get in the way of criticism.

and immediacy which resemble the Tolstoyan and are, perhaps, only surpassed in English by the Shakespearian. The one important respect in which, however, *Troilus and Criseyde* more resembles a great Tolstoyan novel than a Shakespearian play is in the leisureliness of its build-up. A Shakespearian play works at a much greater pressure. Under the 'strong necessity of Time' events of the greatest magnitude and import are compelled into the 'two hours' traffick' of the Elizabethan theatre, and every phrase spoken on the stage had to count enormously, even if there were not other reasons, as no doubt there were, for that Elizabethan intensification of life. The leisureliness of Chaucer's *Troilus and Criseyde* ought not, however, to blind us from recognizing the complexity and value of the organism which is thus gradually built up.

We may start, as literary criticism should, from a consideration of the language of *Troilus and Criseyde*, by simply noting those passages where the English of the poem is most creatively alive and its characteristic strength is revealed. We shall find that they are invariably the passages which present scenes and dialogues in the comedy of Pandarus or Criseyde or both, when both in their association as uncle and niece are present, or, sometimes, when Pandarus is present with Troilus.

The trio and their story were, we know, pre-existent in Boccaccio's *Il Filostrato*.[1] But Chaucer's *Troilus and Criseyde* is a complete re-creation in English. It is enough to recapitulate the superficial differences to recognize that there must be others more radical arising from the differences between Boccaccio's Italian sensibility and Chaucer's English sensibility. Chaucer's version is not only about half as long again as Boccaccio's but the distribution of the emphasis is entirely different. The greater part of Boccaccio's poem dwells on the period after Cressida's departure from Troy, and the intensities of tormented passion in the

---

[1] Earlier still the story had originated as a sketchy episode, one of the mediaeval elaborations on the *historia* of Troy, in Benoît de Saint-Maure's *Roman de Troie*.

poem sound personal, as indeed they probably were. Chaucer, on the other hand, devotes the greater part of his poem to the detached, but profoundly charitable, presentation, as scenes of the human comedy, of the growth and involvements of the love of Troilus and Criseyde in relation to the contrasting character of Pandarus. Pandarus and Criseyde, in Chaucer's poem, are re-creations which, in effect, are new English creations, new creations of Chaucer's English; their life, and that of the poem, is that of the English language. It is in this respect that C. S. Lewis's account of *Troilus and Criseyde* is misleading. What Chaucer does to *Il Filostrato*, according to Lewis, is to mediaevalize that (perhaps) early Renaissance Italian poem. He renders it, if not as an *allegory* of love, at least in the spirit of Guillaume's part of the *Roman de la Rose*. This account is partially accurate, accurate just so far as it goes. Chaucer's Troilus is indeed more like the lover of the *Roman de la Rose* than Boccaccio's Italian gallant. But it certainly does not account for the re-created Pandarus nor re-created Criseyde and therefore does not go very far towards accounting for the English poem; for it is *this* Pandarus and *this* Criseyde who produce the greatest modification in the re-created poem. Lewis's account reads almost as if Chaucer had rendered Boccaccio's Italian into Guillaume's French. There is a radical difference, arising from the difference between the two languages, between the *Roman de la Rose* and *Troilus and Criseyde*.

The basic role of Pandarus may correspond, as Lewis says it does, to that of Frend in the *Romaunt of the Rose*. But the Pandarus of *Troilus and Criseyde* has the organic complexity of a living person as Frend has not. He is also an entirely different person from Boccaccio's Pandaro. There is nothing to choose between Boccaccio's Pandaro and his friend, Troilo, a pair of young Italian gallants, men about a fourteenth-century Italian town. The ripe elderly gentleman who is Criseyde's uncle in Chaucer's English poem is a huge comic creation who contrasts with the serious youthful lover Troilus is.

The English Criseyde is almost as different from her Italian counterpart as Pandarus from his and is a complex life. If we try to analyse this complexity of Criseyde we can trace a little of it back to a diversity of literary origins. She may partially be granted to be (as Lewis much too simply says she is) the courtly lady of the Rose. But she partially originates also in the woman of the *fabliaux*. Some of her ambiguity appears to depend on this dual origination. But of course she goes far beyond either. She moves and talks through varying scenes and situations with the life of a living person, and as such completely transcends both the conventional lady of courtly love and the *fabliau* wife. She does not fit into the courtly love convention, not merely because of the *fabliau* element in her composition, but because she has grown altogether too real to do so. The urgency of her English life has liberated her. Her final faithlessness to Troilus is a faithlessness also to the whole courtly convention. She simply will not be compressed into that frame. The poet may even have felt a little the discourtesy of showing it to be so, if the *Legend of Good Women* is to be taken seriously as his penance. But once the humanness of Criseyde has been so completely realized in the poem as it is, her natural human frailty is correspondingly accepted with all charitableness and forgiveness and her tragedy is as much pitied as that of the self-pitying Troilus.

Troilus is the least Chaucerian of the trio. He retains, and to a considerable extent remains, the conventional outline of the disconsolate trouvère or Petrarchan courtly lover, the complaining, swooning knight (brave though he is in *battle*). To put it in more strictly literary critical terms, the characteristic strength of English is less called into play in his depiction than in the creations of Pandarus and Criseyde.

But the characters ought no longer in this way to be taken for inspection outside the poem. They are elements, distinct values in the poem, the one a criticism of the other.

The first scene is in a temple when Troilus first sees Criseyde. The occasion is the spring festival.

> And so bifel, whan comen was the tyme
> Of Aperil, whan clothed is the mede
> With newe grene, of lusty Ver the pryme.

The temple corresponds here, as Lewis interprets it, to the garden of the Rose. But behind the image of Criseyde 'in widwes habite blak' there already hovers another image, the *fabliau* image of the profane widow in church. Criseyde as we first see her is already poised somewhere ambiguously between the lady of the Rose and the Wife of Bath at the funeral of her fourth husband. Nearer the former, certainly, to begin with.[1]

Throughout the scene in the temple in *Troilus and Criseyde* there is perceptible an ironic interplay of sacred and profane themes (not unlike that in the presentation of the Prioresse in the Canterbury Prologue). There had entered the temple

> . . . so many a lusty knight,
> So many a lady fresh and mayden bright.

The tone of youthful delight certainly resembles that of the garden of the Rose. The occasion was, as Chaucer fully allows, a Pagan festival in Troy, the 'sensual music' dominant. But the human comedy of the scene which develops depends for its particular irony on its being at the same time a very human scene observed in a mediaeval church. Criseyde attracts attention and comment because of her beauty. Her concealment under 'hir blake wede'

> . . . under cloude blak so bright a sterre

is itself equivocal, a reservation of hidden power; and her

---

[1] Criseyde is realized entirely on the human plane and never acquires an added symbolical value as Beatrice does on the occasion in the *Vita Nuova* when Dante sees her in a church.

humility of demeanour may not be, or may not wholly be, a devotional humility, but a womanly bashfulness arising from her consciousness of her femininity in the presence of a company of young knights.

> And yet she stood ful lowe and stille alloon,
> Bihinden othere folk, in litel brede,
> And neigh the dore, ay under shames drede,
> Simple of a-tyr . . .

She is fearful but at the same time sure of herself, conscious of the power of her beauty.

> With ful assured loking and manere.

Yet Chaucer's English Criseyde has a primal freshness of innocence, as of life springing into light from the source. In this respect she differs from the typical *fabliau* wife who is a type evolved by the satires against women. Her secrecy is not a conscious sly bait, her humility not a pious disguise but a natural womanly modesty. It is because in Chaucer's English she is so alive that she is beginning to move in the direction of that other Chaucerian creation, the Wife of Bath, who is herself so much more than a *fabliau* wife.

With Troilus also, as he leads his 'yonge knightes' up and down in the temple

> Biholding ay the ladyes of the toun,

the religious observances seem to be secondary to the profane interest in women. Although he as yet owes 'devocioun' to none, he is in the same phase, we may agree, as the young man entering the garden in the *Roman de la Rose*. If he observed the eyes of any knight or squire in his company light on any woman,

> He wolde smyle, and holden it folye.

Thereby in his pride of youthful ignorance, he offends the god of Love. His mockery of 'Love's servants' sounds more like Jean de Meung than Guillaume de Lorris

And seye him thus, 'god wot, she slepeth softe
For love of thee, whan thou tornest ful ofte!'

but has not been earned by his experience and is double-
edged; for the nemesis of Troilus' proud attitude of
superiority to love is imminent. 'Withinne the temple . . .
pleying' he himself is struck—transfixed into a lover—
the instant his eyes light on Criseyde. We must just accept
the convention that Troilus, as a courtly lover, was there
and then committed to secrecy. (Special motives are indeed
suggested for this enforcement to secrecy in Troilus' case.
But the rule was, as stated in the *De Amore* of Andreas
Capellanus, the mediaeval textbook of love, *Qui non celat,
amare non potest*.) The situation, as Lewis takes pains to
point out, is a conventional situation—if to fall in love
quite naturally is a conventional situation.

For the point surely is that the conventional situation is
quite transformed and transcended by Chaucer's knowledge of the heart and profound humanity. The woman-
liness of Criseyde,

> . . . creature
> Was never lasse mannish in seminge,

her perfection as a womanly creature and total human
naturalness of demeanour are so beautifully apprehended
that the effect on Troilus is realized as the most natural
thing in the world.

> (He) Gan for to lyke hir mening and hir chere,
>   Which somdel deynous was, for she leet falle
>   Hir look a lite a-side, in swich manere,
>   Ascaunces, 'what! may I not stonden here?'

Love is engendered in the eyes

>   And of hir look in him ther gan to quiken,
>   So greet desir, and swich affeccioun,
>   That in his hertes botme gan to stiken
>   Of hir his fixe and depe impressioun

although Troilus

> Was ful unwar that love hadde his dwellinge
> With-inne the subtile stremes of hir yën.

The birth of love is here realized with an awareness of the self that the seventeenth-century metaphysical love poetry only extends and elaborates. The perception is already here.

The first entrance of Pandarus is to Troilus disconsolate in his room. Pandarus at once makes his presence felt as a living commonsensical personality with a good dash of the goliard in his composition. He is the advocate of 'jolytee' and 'lustinesse', and treats 'holinesse' with disrespect.

> God save hem that bi-seged han our toun,
> And so can leye our jolytee on presse,
> And bring our lusty folk to holinesse!

He affects to mistake the cause of his friend's trouble with the humane purpose of inducing him to expose his secret, for he understands human nature very well, and, having a more than usual share of human warmth, wants to help. Yet despite his riper worldly wisdom Pandarus has to occupy a status in the story subordinate to Troilus. As a *persona* of the human comedy he grows more alive and real than Troilus. Yet to keep him fitted into his role he is necessarily defined as an inferior, a comedian, his familiarity not breeding respect. He is made game of as being himself inexpert and hopelessly unsuccessful in love.

> Thou coudest never in love thy-selven wisse;
> How devel maystow bringen me to blisse?

Troilus dismisses his practical wisdom of 'proverbes' and 'olde ensamples'

> Nor other cure canstow noon for me
> Eek I nil not be cured, I wol deye;
> What knowe I of the quene Niobe?
> Lat be thyne olde ensaumples, I thee preye.

Yet it may be observed that Troilus is here disclosing his own drooping proclivity ('Eek I nil not be cured, I wol deye') which the very presence of Pandarus in the poem establishes a robust criticism of. Pandarus' 'proverbes', in so far as they are taken alive out of contemporary spoken English, are part of a living traditional wisdom of human experience, and even his bookish pedantry, his 'olde ensaumples', is an element that either by contrast or assimilation enriches the total comic verve of his colloquial English.

3

It is in the vivid scenes of the second book, in their mutual society as uncle and niece, that Pandarus and Criseyde unfold. Criseyde seen only at a distance in the temple in the first book is now seen in the domestic intimacy of her own house as she converses with her uncle. At the moment of Pandarus' entrance she and two other women, themselves enclosed in a besieged city, are listening to the tale of another siege, the tale of Thebes, being read to them by a maid. Noticing the book, and expressing courteous regret for his interruption, Pandarus asks

> 'For goddes love, what seith it? tel it us.
> Is it of love? O, some good ye me lere!'
> 'Uncle,' quod she, 'your maistresse is not here!'

With that they gonnen laughe . . .

In the merriment that breaks out so unconstrainedly between them there is at once the clash of two distinctly realized individuals. Criseyde and her ladies take their stand firmly against the frivolity of love on the side of the serious business of war. But the battle of wit is only a mock battle. There is a deep congeniality of temperament between uncle and niece; they share the same idiom, an idiom that can be disrespectful in tone towards a great public man, a bishop, who has just at the moment of Pandarus' entrance come to grief in the book.

> How the bisshop, as the book can telle,
> Amphiorax, fil thurgh the ground to helle.

Pandarus lightly dismisses the tiresome historical book altogether and asks his niece how she is.

> Quod Pandarus, 'al this knowe I myselve,
> And al th'assege of Thebes and the care;
> For her-of been ther maked bokes twelve;—
> But lat be this, and tel me how ye fare.'

He thus sets immediate, particular and personal human values in place of a historical past built up by clerkly authorities in books and weighting the present political obsession. He bids her do observance to May, Love's festival month.

> Do wey your book, rys up, and lat us daunce,
> And lat us don to May som observaunce.

Pandarus is here a messenger of life, the impulsive joy of the natural heart in the spring as opposed to the clerk's pedantry and the widow's nun-like seclusion. His proffer of a renewal of the possibilities of life appeals to Criseyde, as the strained note in her overemphatic response betrays.

> It sete me wel bet ay in a cave
> To bidde, and rede on holy seyntes lyves:
> Lat maydens gon to daunce, and yonge wyves.

Her exaggeration of holiness and protestation of outraged propriety turn, perhaps not unconsciously on the high-spirited young woman's own part, to near-burlesque. Pandarus tells her that he knows something that would be great news to her if she knew. To anyone shut up in a besieged city such news could only mean, it might be supposed, one thing; and very naturally Criseyde exclaims

> For goddes love, is than th'assege aweye?
> I am of Grekes so ferd that I deye.

58

The ironies involved with Criseyde's fearfulness here are that she herself is on the point of being besieged, and (for an audience who know the story) that it was a Greek, Diomede, who finally won her. Pandarus having aroused his niece's curiosity provokingly withholds the satisfaction of it. But, as if by chance, he introduces Troilus' name and p aises, and he repeats his earlier appeal.

> But yet I seye, aryseth, lat us daunce,
> And cast your widwes habit to mischaunce:
> What list yow thus your-self to disfigure?

The life-likeness of Pandarus' leave-taking from his niece is such that it is as if the artistic medium in which it is conveyed has been quite consumed away and we are confronted with the thing itself. Pandarus is on the point at last, at the very end of his visit, of dislosing the identity of her lover.

> With that she gan hir eyen doun to caste,
> And Pandarus to coghe gan a lyte.

That moment of embarrassment appears to include the mutual recognition that it is the moment of Destiny for Criseyde ('this matere is so bihovely'). The social detachment and reticences have given way; uncle and niece have moved into the sphere of a closer intimacy. Yet, when he gazes too long on her face—pondering on whether or not she will be one of the lucky ones—she asks with some of her old assurance

> Sey ye me never er now?

Under the shock of Pandarus's revelation that the young prince is her lover, and his eloquent plea to her heart for pity—to which he adds the eternal plea of the brevity of life and the reminder that beauty succumbs to Elde— Criseyde's formality of decorous and pious widowhood begins to melt; for Criseyde is exceedingly tender-hearted. Yet her frailties and refuges of self-deceit are at the same time tenderly exposed in the clear, though gentle, light of Chaucerian contemplation.

> And if this man slee here him-self, allas!
> In my presence, it wol be no solas.
> What men wold of hit deme . . .

> 'Can he wel speke of love?' quod she, 'I preye,
> Tel me, for I the bet me shal purveye' . . .

> For man may love, of possibilitee,
> A womman, so, his herte may to-breste,
> And she nought love ayein, but if her leste . . .

We see here that the lady of the Rose's extreme fearfulness for her reputation and her consciousness of her privilege to give or withhold her favour may have a comic aspect. But if an element of the satire on women found in Jean de Meung is present, Criseyde's wonderful livingness as she moves in the human comedy arises from Chaucer's profounder and more charitable knowledge.

Pandarus's visit is succeeded by the scene in which Troilus himself—'so lyke a man of armes and a knight'— rides up the street which Criseyde's house overlooks and brings her to her window. The moment corresponds for Criseyde to the moment in the temple for Troilus. Spectacular as the scene is, it is again on the human emotions involved that the attention is centred, and particularly on the effect on Criseyde's heart. We preparatorily glimpse the state in which Pandarus has left that heart.

> But straught in-to hir closet wente anoon,
> And sette here doun as stille as any stoon,
> And every word gan up and doun to winde.

She is roused from her thought.

> But as she sat allone and thoughte thus,
> The'ascry aroos at skarmish al with-oute,
> And men cryde in the strete, 'see, Troilus
> Hath right now put to flight the Grekes route!'

With that gan al hir meynee for to shoute,
'A! go we see, caste up the latis wyde;
For thurgh this strete he moot to palays ryde;

For other wey is fro the yate noon
Of Dardanus, ther open is the cheyne.'
With that com he and al his folk anoon
An esy pas rydinge, in routes tweyne,
Right as his happy day was, sooth to seyne,
For which, men say, may nought disturbed be
That shal bityden of necessitee.

This Troilus sat on his baye stede,
Al armed, save his heed, ful richely,
And wounded was his hors, and gan to blede,
On whiche he rood a pas, ful softely;
But swich a knightly sighte, trewely,
As was on him, was nought, with-outen faile,
To loke on Mars, that god is of batayle . . .

His helm to-hewen was in twenty places,
That by a tissew heng, his bak bihinde,
His sheld to-dasshed was with swerdes and maces,
In which men mighte many an arwe finde
That thirled hadde horn and nerf and rinde;
And ay the peple cryde, 'here cometh our joye,
And, next his brother, holdere up of Troye!'

For which he wex a litel reed for shame,
Whan he the peple up-on him herde cryen,
That to biholde it was a noble game,
How sobreliche he caste doun his yën.
Criseyde gan al his chere aspyen,
And leet so softe it in hir herte sinke,
That to hir-self she seyde, 'who yaf me drinke?'

The gentle humanness of Troilus—'an esy pas rydinge'—
contrasts with his role as victorious warrior, associate of
Mars. Even his horse is almost human, not just a picture

of a horse but a wounded life. This Chaucerian humanity, even on a great scenic occasion, is revealed particularly in the naturalness of Troilus' demeanour in response to the shouts of the crowd, a modesty in the youthful hero that might be the bashfulness of a lover, and finally most dramatically in the effect on Criseyde—'who yaf me drinke?'[1]

In the debate whether or not to yield to love which thereafter Criseyde secretly has with herself, we seem to hear the accents of the Wife of Bath; it is the familiar English talking-idiom responding to her inner thoughts.

> I knowe also, and alday here and see,
> Men loven wommen al this toun aboute;
> Be they the wers? why, nay, with-outen doute . . .
>
> Ne me to love, a wonder is it nought;
> For wel wot I my-self, so god me spede,
> Al wolde I that noon wiste of this thought,
> I am oon the fayreste, out of drede,
> And goodlieste, who-so taketh hede;
> And so men seyn in al the toun of Troye.
> What wonder is it though he of me have joye?
>
> I am myn owene woman, wel at ese,
> I thanke it god, as after myn estat;
> Right yong, and stonde unteyd in lusty lese,
> With-outen jalousye or swich debat;
> Shal noon housbonde seyn to me 'chekmat!'
> For either they ben ful of jalousye,
> Or maisterful, or loven novelrye.
>
> What shal I doon? to what fyn live I thus?
> Shal I nat loven, in cas if that me leste?
> What, par dieux! I am nought religious!

Criseyde is here by no means simply the lady of the Rose.

[1] Some of our Chaucer editors would like us to believe that 'drinke' here means a 'love potion'. I see no reason to think that what is meant is other than simply that the effect on Criseyde was like that of a glass of wine.

As a complex living woman she walks 'pleyinge' into her garden, no longer an allegorical garden, though it does retain some of the quality of the allegorical garden of the Rose. Her three nieces, Flexippe, Tharbe and Antigone, and her company of attendant women, have replaced the personifications and goddesses of the allegorical garden but still accord her a ceremonial, processional dignity of young spring-like life. Antigone's song and, later, the nightingale's in the cedar (an image from the Italian landscape of love) further dispose her to love, and her dream makes clear what has in fact happened to her.

Pandarus pays a second visit to his niece. He bears a letter which he has himself instructed Troilus to compose —with a bit of advice that is rather in the spirit of Ovid than of Guillaume de Lorris.

> Biblotte it with thy teres eek a lyte.

At his entrance he first obtrudes his own incurable passion.

> I may not slepe never a Mayes morwe;
> I have a joly wo, a lusty sorwe.

But Pandarus' woe is 'joly', his sorrow 'lusty'.

> 'Now by your feyth, myn uncle,' quod she, 'dere,
> What maner windes gydeth yow now here?
> Tel us your joly wo and your penaunce,
> How ferforth be ye put in loves daunce.'

> 'By god,' quod he, 'I hoppe alwey bihinde!'
> And she to-laugh, it thoughte hir herte breste,
> Quod Pandarus, 'loke alwey that ye finde
> Game in myn hood . . .'

The phantastic image of Pandarus as a ship guided by the wind sets the comic tone, and shifts easily into the other image of Pandarus fallen behind in love's dance—'I hoppe alwey bihinde'. He is seen for a moment, by his own self-caricature, as the parodying clown, the satyr whose clumsy movements burlesque the delicate movements of the ex·

63

pert dancers. Yet uncle and niece talk easily together with
the freedom of a shared humanity and of a social world
in common.

> With that they wenten arm in arm y-fere
> In-to the gardin from the chaumbre doun.

(With Troilus also Pandarus is socially quite an equal, on
easy terms as a familiar friend, though from their association a contrast of attitude and character is what emerges.)
After the serious, tense talk in the garden where he passes
to her the letter, Pandarus again releases the buffoon in
himself, evoking Criseyde's mirth at his own expense and
by his goliardic irreverence.

> Therewith she lough, and seyde, 'go we dyne'.
> And he gan at him-self to jape faste,
> And seyde, 'nece, I have so greet a pyne
> For love that every other day I faste'—
> And gan his beste japes forth to caste;
> And made hir so to laughe at his folye,
> That she for laughter wende for to dye.

The lady of the Rose could scarcely be thought of as
laughing so freely with Pandarus. When Criseyede re-
appears, after reading Troilus' letter in the privacy of her
chamber, we may judge by her boisterous renewal of
'game' with her uncle that she has not been altogether dis-
pleased by its contents.

> Er he was war, she took him by the hood,
> And seyde, 'ye were caught er that ye wiste'.

In point of fact it is she who is caught. These are the gam-
bollings of a creature unconsciously caught in the con-
trivances of Pandarus and Fortune ('But god and Pan-
dare wiste al what this mente.').

4

The union of the lovers is accomplished and celebrated

in the third book. The equivocalness (I feel) of this not perfectly orchestrated third book arises from the mutual presence of incompatible courtly love and *fabliau* elements. These have not been entirely transcended and in places their conjunction seems incomplete and jars. Criseyde, from tender-heartedness, yields to Pandarus' pleadings on behalf of his love-sick friend so far as to visit Troilus' bedside as his physician (his 'leche'), and to save his life accepts him as her 'servaunt'. This is quite in accordance with the spirit of courtly love. But the narration, at a later stage of the same book, of how the lovers are more or less pushed into bed together by Pandarus has the quite different character of a farcical *fabliau* intrigue. Yet it is not the equivocalness arising from this conjunction, but the 'failure of the conjunction' itself, the falling apart of the disparate elements, that is felt to be unsatisfactory. Equivocalness itself is, perhaps, in the very essence of human experience;[1] and the reader is betrayed into these circumstances very much as Criseyde herself is betrayed; however humanitarian or commonsensical may be her uncle's motives, his duplicity in this episode is fox-like.

The delightful carefree supper party—

> He sang; she pleyed; he tolde tale of Wade—

at Pandarus' house, the betrayer's house, is again a version of the earthly paradise which is not without its serpent or (as in Chauntecleer's case) fox.[2] Fortune sends the 'smoky

---

[1] Arising from the subjective-objective antithesis.

[2] The betrayal theme runs through the poem. Criseyde's father, Calkas, is a traitor—'him that falsely hadde his feith so broken' . . . 'hir fadres shame, his falseness and tresoun'. By her exchange for Antenor a traitor is introduced into the town. She recognizes her uncle as a traitor to her and he recognizes himself as a traitor to his niece. When he falsely tells Criseyde that Troilus fancies she is false to him there is unconscious irony in her protestations.

> Horaste! allas! and falsen Troilus . . .
> Now god, thou wost, in thought ne dede untrewe
> To Troilus was never yet Criseyde.

Criseyde's faithlessness to Troilus is the supreme instance; but Criseyde

reyne' which detains Criseyde for the fatal night in her uncle's house where Troilus lurks. At that point, the point at which Fortune directly intervenes, the poem takes on a deeper seriousness, a seriousness that a little later issues in Criseyde's Boethian meditation on the impermanence of human felicity. It is as if Criseyde's felicity were about to be ended. Yet the union of Criseyde and Troilus, once accomplished, is celebrated as a joyous epithalamion, transcending the dubiousness of the preliminaries. The ecstasy of human love is rendered in theological terms, as the soul new risen from purgatory.

> Thus sondry peynes bringen folk to hevene . . .
> For out of wo in blisse now they flete . . .

The use of theological terms here, the most precise available to distinguish psychological states, does not imply any identification, much less confusion of the human with the divine. It was the allegorical method to describe one plane of being in terms of another without blurring the distinction between the two. Scholastic verbal habits are a distinction of mediaeval literature, and the poetry of courtly love had long been in the habit of borrowing theological terminology. When Troilus utters the joy of human love in the words of Dante's hymn to the Virgin it is no more incongruous in its context than is the typical Dawn Song that appropriately terminates the night.

It is the sudden shift produced by Pandarus' visit to his niece the morning after that rudely places the lovers' rapture and at the same time places Pandarus. The broad ribald quality of Pandarus' joviality in this dialogue has an effect of painful disenchantment coming where it does (as Juliet's Nurse in *Romeo and Juliet*, simply the old peasant woman, has not). The coarse *fabliau* element in Pandarus comes to the surface.

> Seyde, 'al this night so reyned it, allas!

---

herself has been betrayed first by her uncle and again by Diomede's wooing. Finally, the fickleness of Fortune undoes all.

That al my drede is that ye, nece swete,
Han litel layser had to slepe and mete;
Al night', quod he, 'hath reyn so do me wake,
That som of us, I trowe, hir hedes ake.'

And ner he com, and seyde, 'how stont it now
This mery morwe, nece, how can ye fare?'
Criseyde answerde, 'never the bet for yow,
Fox that ye been, god yeve your herte care!
God helpe me so, ye caused al this fare,
Trow I,' quod she, 'for alle your wordes whyte;
O! who-so seeth yow knoweth yow ful lyte!'

With that she gan hir face for to wrye
With the shete, and wex for shame al reed;
And Pandarus gan under for to prye,
And seyde, 'nece, if that I shal ben deed,
Have here a swerd, and smyteth of myn heed.'
With that his arm al sodeynly he thriste
Under hir nekke, and at the laste hir kiste.

The fox image springs from the rustic-comic beast-fable source. As an image of the betrayer it merges into the progressive disenchantment, the succession of betrayals, as it might be called, which is an element in the process of the poem. The deterioration of Pandarus as a moral character here—his grossness brought to notice and the suggestion of his need for vicarious compensation for his own failure in love—is not what is being primarily contemplated but, like the moral and physical deterioration of Falstaff in *Henry the Fourth*, Part Two, is itself an aspect of the poem's development. An element of the actual that the idealism of courtly love would have ignored or, at least, has failed perfectly to assimilate, is felt as brutal fact in the painful disenchantment of its obtrusion in this context.

Yet, after this scene the joyous celebration of human love is resumed, though with a difference, and dominates the close of this book. Troilus' Boethian song to Love celebrates a conception of Love as 'the great bond of things', a unifying, creative power associated with Nature. It is inclusive of both the courtly and the *fabliau* attitudes and it transcends both. Though the love celebrated is the love of the creature, that love, as now conceived, is so completely inclusive that it could itself be transcended only by the love of the Creator, or—since the love of the Creator may be conceived as inclusive of the love of the creature— by the love of the whole.

5

Fortune, which united the lovers in the third book, cuts short their felicity in the fourth. Fortune here plays a part not dissimilar to that of Time in Shakespeare's *Troilus and Cressida*, the symbolic agent of the break-up in the moral-social order. Personal human relationships are felt as fragile indeed in relation to Time in Shakespeare's *Troilus and Cressida* (as D. A. Traversi has shown); the rather ill-matched lovers are no sooner brought together than the next moment they are again forced apart by the rude action of Time. The mediaeval Fortune has nothing of this terrible intensity of Elizabethan Time.

> Devouring Time, blunt thou the lion's paws,

Time associated with Death's dissolution of the body.[1] Human affairs as they unfold are contemplated calmly in Chaucer, although within the temporary jurisdiction of the fickle goddess.

The reversal of fortune in the fourth book has a human agent, this time not Pandarus but Calkas; for it is Calkas who arranges the unfortunate withdrawal of his daughter from the doomed city. This 'olde greye' pathetically desires to have his daughter; yet he is felt as having other aspects of the character of Elde, a character envious of youth and love, and also covetous—

[1] And not only the human body but the body politic.

> Desyr of gold shal so his sowle blende.

We find Criseyde attempting to counter this inimical spirit of Elde; warding off, with her disrespect, her father's sacred foreknowledge.

> For goddes speken in amphibologyes,
> And, for a sooth, they tellen twenty lyes.

But she is in his power and it seems more than man's.

The main themes of the fourth book are dramatized as the attitudes of Troilus, Pandarus, Criseyde to the stroke of Fortune. The grief-struck condition of Troilus is presented in one or two sharp (and complex) images.

> Y-bounden in the blake bark of care . . .
> Ful lyk a deed image pale and wan . . .

Pandarus, visiting his friend upon the unexpected collapse of the lovers' paradise he had so cunningly contrived, is momentarily himself a spectacle almost as pitiable as the pitiable spectacle he confronts.

> In-to the derke chaumbre, as stille as stoon,
> Toward the bed gan softely to goon
> So confus, that he niste what to seye;
> For verray wo his wit was neigh aweye.

But, never long at a loss, he recovers himself and offers such commonsensical, and unsuitable, advice as that the 'toun is ful of ladies al aboute' and Troilus may lightly choose another.

> If oon can singe, another can wel daunce.

In the dialogue that follows the temporarily roused Troilus meets Pandarus on his own ground in the same lively colloquial idiom.

> But canstow pleyen raket to and fro
> Nette in, dokke out, now this, now that, Pandare.

He compares Pandarus to a man who, seeing another in torment, says to him

> Thenk not on smert, and thou shalt fele noon.

But Troilus relapses again into grief-struck passivity. The sophistications of his courtly idealism withhold him from employing the discourtesy of force to keep his lady in Troy. From the contrary standpoint of Pandarus' advice to act from downright self-interest—

> Devyne not a reson ay so depe
> Ne curteysly, but help thy-self anoon—

these scruples are 'nyce vanitee'.

But the great scene in the fourth book, a scene in which the comedy changes unawares, yet before our eyes, into the other reality of tragedy, is the scene in which Criseyde's women friends in Troy pay her a visit to say good-bye. In the fineness of its observation of social behaviour, the living naturalness of its dialogue (in these respects it is a forerunner of the great tea parties, and such occasions, of the novel and the drama), and above all in the alteration produced by the knowledge and revelation of the heart, it is one of the great human scenes in *Troilus and Criseyde*. The point of the irony, and at the same time of the pity, is in the collision between the public, social life and the private, secret life of the heart. The women come to sympathize or rejoice with Criseyde according to whichever they may feel to be the more tactful, but they fail to comprehend, because they do not know, cannot penetrate the secret inner life of Criseyde's heart. They sympathize but for the inappropriate reasons, assuming a different cause for the strange grief that in the end, when the social comedy turns for Criseyde into unendurable irony, they have to notice.

> But as men seen in toune, and al aboute,
> That wommen usen frendes to visyte,
> So to Criseyde of wommen com a route

For pitous joye, and wenden hir delyte;
And with hir tales, dere y-nough a myte,
These wommen, whiche that in the cite dwelle,
They sette hem doun, and seyde as I shal telle.

Quod first that oon, 'I am glad, trewely,
By-cause of yow, that shal your fader see.'
A-nother seyde, 'y-wis, so nam not I;
For al to litel hath she with us be.'
Quod tho the thridde, 'I hope, y-wis, that she
Shal bringen us the pees on every syde,
That, whan she gooth, almighty god hir gyde!'

Tho wordes and tho wommannisshe thinges,
She herde hem right as though she thennes were;
For, god it wot, hir herte on other thing is,
Although the body sat among hem there.
Hir advertence is alwey elles-where;
For Troilus ful faste hir soule soughte;
With-outen word, alwey on him she thoughte . . .

The first two lines invoke social form and good custom. The 'route of wommen' are performing a social rite for 'pitous joye'—sorry she must leave them, glad for her sake that she will see her father so soon, and perhaps glad also simply because they enjoy paying visits. There is no escaping them—'they sette hem doun'—however indisposed Criseyde is for such a visit. They say at once what they intend as all the appropriate tactful things that are said on such an occasion. The background of the public misfortune inevitably inserts itself in the course of these polite, good-natured remarks, and Criseyde's departure is related to the hope of a favourable turn in the political situation.

> 'I hope, y-wis, that she
> Shal bringen us the pees on every syde. . . .'

Criseyde's private grief being to her at that moment overwhelming, this concern for the public good only aggra-

vates the irony. Then, our attention is shifted to the heart
of Criseyde.

> Tho wordes and tho wommanisshe thinges,
> She herde hem right as though she thennes were.

There is presented—in the midst of all this solicitude—
the absent mind,

> For, god it wot, hir herte on other thing is,
> Although the body sat among hem there,

the preoccupied heart for which social tact and sympathy,
uncomprehending and unknowing, are without relevance.
The climax is reached when Criseyde, unable to endure
the ironic tension longer, breaks down in tears and they
can only suppose with engaging egoism that she weeps
because she must part from Troy and themselves. They
weep, too, not knowing what they are weeping for. The
scene is placed as 'vanitee'—'after al this nyce vanitee'.
The implication seems to be, not only that the women's
sociable sympathy is ineffectual, missing the point, but
perhaps also that their whole lives and conversation are
'vain'.

6

The fifth and last book, the book of Troilus parted from
Criseyde and finally deserted, is *predominantly* a prolonged
musical lament—the music peculiarly unforced, no strain,
no sense of effort disturbing the outflow of Troilus' gentle
giving tongue to grief. The lady herself proving in the end
faithless, this book is the swan-song of courtly love. It
opens with the scene of Criseyde's sorrowful departure
from Troy escorted by Troilus with the ceremonial accom-
paniment of a hundred knights to beyond the walls where
Troilus takes farewell of her. Thereafter 'this sodeyn Diomede', while acting as her escort to her father's tent in the
foreign camp, is insolently quick to seize the advantage.

Troilus, parted from Criseyde, now begins to have substantial cause for grief, and the fact that his complainings are so musically, if diffusely, rendered argues an imaginative sympathy—at least their rejection by the judgment is held deliberately in suspension during this prolonged musical utterance. Pandarus' humorous commonsensical presence, though that presence appropriately recedes somewhat in the last book, continues to qualify the sympathy. His continued juxtaposition with Troilus in these final scenes produces a balance of sympathy and un-sympathy with Troilus and with the whole courtly convention which is felt to have got, in Troilus' case, perhaps a little out of hand.

Already in the fourth book, supervening on the commonsense of his debate with Pandarus, Troilus' trick of 'fantasye' breaks wantonly loose at what is still only the prospect of parting and there are heard the opening bars of that fuller melancholy music that is heard again more sustainedly in the last book. It is in the production of this music that the English of the poem may be felt in passages to be modified by the music of the Latin languages, the Latin music of Ovid's deserted heroines of the *Heroides*, Boccaccio's Italian music of passionate lament in *Il Filostrato*, and more occasionally by the graver music of the *Inferno*.

> . . . but doun with Proserpyne,
> Whan I am deed, I wol go wone in pyne;
> And there I wol eternally compleyne
> My wo, and how that twinned be we tweyne.

Criseyde herself is caught up momentarily, later in the fourth book, in this operatic ritualization of grief. Reassuming the trappings of woe, the black of widowhood—

> . . . my clothes everichoon
> Shal blake been . . .

she fancifully anticipates her role with Troilus among the shades.

> For though in erthe y-twinned be we tweyne,
> Yet in the field of pitee, out of peyne,
> That hight Elysos . . .
> As Orpheus and Erudice . . .

But Criseyde is here momentarily moving outside her own characteristic idiom, and unlike Troilus does not in the last book sustain this slightly foreign or Spenserian music.

Yet Troilus' musical complainings in some of their exaggeration even in the last book, where they have increasingly substantial cause, are not free from suggestions of caricature which mark them as exaggerated.

> And graspe aboute I may, but in this place,
> Save a pilowe, I find noght t'embrace.

The gravity of that image—bearing in mind the presence of Pandarus in the background, and also perhaps the consideration that the prospect before Troilus is as yet only a ten days' separation if Criseyde were to prove true as he evidently had no right to suppose she would not—the gravity of that image is not so secure as, in its context in the *Legend*, that of Ariadne deserted.

> She gropeth in the bedde, and fond right noght.

The addition of that 'save a pilowe' tilts the balance.

Troilus gives Pandarus instructions for his funeral, a little prematurely, for the arrangement still is that Criseyde shall reappear at the end of the ten days.

> But of the fyr and flaumbe funeral
> In whiche my body brenne shal to glede,
> And of the feste and pleys palestral
> At my vigile, I pray thee take good hede
> That al be wel; and offre Mars my stede,
> My swerd, myn helm, and, leve brother dere,
> My sheld to Pallas, that shyneth clere.
>
> The poudre in which myn herte y-brend shal torne
> That preye I thee thou take and it conserve

In a vessel, that men clepeth an urne,
Of gold, and to my lady that I serve,
For love of whom thus pitously I sterve,
So yeve it hir, and do me this plesaunce,
To preye hir kepe it for a remembraunce.

For wel I fele, by my maladye,
And by my dremes now and yore ago,
Al certeinly, that I mot nedes dye.
The owle eek, which that hight Ascaphilo,
Hath after me shright alle thise nightes two.
And, god Mercurie! of me now, woful wrecche,
The soule gyde, and, whan thee list, it fecche!

Poetry has here her tragic buskin on. Yet even here the
'rhetoric' is not primarily stylistic, not reducible as pompous diction or figurative extravagance. It is the contemplated mood which in itself is one of such fantastic self-
dramatization—the warrior slain by love—as to tremble
in melancholy panoplied magnificence on the edge of the
comic. The effect of these melancholy heroics, in the
neighbourhood of the Pandarus idiom, is melodramatic,
tragical rather than tragic, the pageantry and posturings
of tragedy without a *motif* sufficiently justified by anything
that has as yet happened. The melting self-pitying mood
which has engendered this histrionic flamboyance has
been encouraged, if not induced, by a convention that has
itself come unfixed from its basis in nature. Pandarus'
common sense stands its ground against this fantastic
and insidious grief; he responds not only with pity but
with common sense.

That it is folye for to sorwen thus,
And causeless . . .
I can not seen in him no remedye,
But lete him worthen with his fantasye.

He asks
If that thou trowe, er this, that any wight
Hath loved paramours as wel as thou?

75

That might indeed be the mature attitude, if it could have been Troilus'—for of course it is easy for Pandarus to talk.

The contrast between Pandarus and Troilus is further dramatized by their attitudes to the dreams and nightmares which Troilus' grief has engendered. Pandarus' attitude corresponds rather to Pertelote's, as Troilus' corresponds rather to Chauntecleer's, in this version of the mediaeval debate on dreams.

> Thy swevenes eek and al swich fantasye
> Dryf out, and lat hem faren to mischaunce;
> For they procede of thy malencolye,
> That doth thee fele in sleep al this penaunce.
> A straw for alle swevenes significaunce!
> God helpe me so, I counte hem not a bene,
> Ther woot no man aright what dremes mene.
>
> For prestes of the temple tellen this,
> That dremes been the revelaciouns
> Of goddes, and as wel they telle, y-wis,
> That they ben infernals illusiouns;
> And leches seyn, that of complexiouns
> Proceden they, or fast, or glotonye.
> Who woot in sooth thus what they signifye?
>
> Eek others seyn that thorugh impressiouns,
> As if a wight hath faste a thing in minde,
> That there-of cometh swiche avisiouns;
> And othere seyn, as they in bokes finde,
> That, after tymes of the yeer by kinde,
> Men dreme, and that th'effect goth by the mone;
> But leve no dream, for it is noght to done.
>
> Wel worth of dremes ay thise olde wyves,
> And treweliche eek augurie of thise foules;
> For fere of which men wenen lese her lyves,
> As ravens qualm, or shryking of thise oules.
> To trowen on it bothe fals and foul is.

> Allas, allas, so noble a creature
> As is a man, shal drede swich ordure!

The clarifying and humane reason is at work, dispersing superstitious fears, promoting a clearer self-knowledge. Pandarus is here a wise, as well as confident, doctor of the mind. We are at the upper limit of his wisdom. His good sense is no negative scepticism, but points outward to a promise of greater self-mastery and a glad acceptance of life.

> Rys, lat us speke of lusty life in Troy.

Pandarus' particular conception of life and enjoyment may be a coarsely mundane one, and not to be identified with the total Chaucerian conception of life. But it is at least preferable, one might be disposed to think, to the self-pitying fantasies on which Troilus feeds his heart.

Yet, from another point of view—the view finally presented in the poem that the only completion of human love is the love of God—Pandarus seeks to guide Troilus backward into the primal garden of the carefree enjoyment of the natural heart from which he started. An impression of it is restored on the occasion of Troilus' visit, accompanied by Pandarus, to Sarpedoun's house party. Through it still perpetually move, dancing, singing, playing, the carolling company of round-cheeked ladies from among whom Criseyde herself originally emerged. But it would be impossible for Troilus, accompanied now by Pandarus, to enter that garden a second time with original innocent delight. The carolling company, Criseyde absent, are now a contrasting background to the complaining grief-stricken lover left solitarily—except for the near presence of Pandarus—in the foreground.

> For she, that of his herte berth the keye,
> Was absent, lo, this was his fantasye,
> That no wight sholde make melodye.

The double signification of 'keye' enriches the meaning unusually for Chaucer. But the significant Chaucerian word here is again that 'fantasye' which, as so often in Chaucer, means a vain imagining.

When released at last (having scrupulously avoided discourtesy to his host) Troilus is on his way home with Pandarus, so strong is the wish in which his 'fantasye' is rooted, that it has induced him to believe that he will find Criseyde, already returned, in her own house. It is indeed at this point that the lover's yearning and sense of loss and vacancy are accorded the tenderest and least qualified sympathy, if we may judge by the sheer beauty of the poetry. Troilus re-visits Criseyde's empty house, haunts the places where in the past, he remembers, she danced, laughed, played and sang. The description of how, standing on the walls, Troilus 'sighed his soul towards the Grecian tents' is perhaps the climax of this phase of the poetry.

> Upon the walles faste eek wold he walke,
> And on the Grekes ost he wolde see,
> And to him-self right thus he wolde talke,
> 'Lo, yonder is myn owne lady free,
> Or elles yonder, there tho tentes be!
> And thennes comth this eyr, that is so sote,
> That in my soule I fele it doth me bote.
>
> And hardely this wind, that more and more
> Thus stoundemele encreseth in my face,
> Is of my ladyes depe sykes sore.
> I preve it thus, for in non othere place
> Of al this toun, save onliche in this space
> Fele I no wind that souneth so lyk peyne;
> It seyth, 'allas! why twinned be we tweyne?'

Though irony underlies its extravagance—Criseyde, we know, will prove faithless—the conceit (for it may be called such) is yet natural, emotionally true and not only fancifully beautiful.

Yet one tends to remember the last book too simply as the book of the sorrow of Troilus deserted. It is predominantly that. But Troilus' behaviour is itself more various than one tends to remember it. At the gate on the tenth day awaiting Criseyde he is, as accompanied by Pandarus, a tragi-comic rather than a tragic figure. There is, for the modern reader, perhaps the shadow of a resemblance here to that other tragi-comic pair, Don Quixote and Sancho Panza. The day passes and she still does not appear. But Troilus is assiduous in inventing reasons and excuses for her delay, and provides only too convincing an instance of the soul's weakness, if the wish is strong, for deluding itself.

> 'I commende hir wysdom, by myn hood!
> She wol not maken peple nycely
> Gaure on hir, whan she comth; but softely
> By nighte in-to the toun she thenketh ryde.
> And, dere brother, thenk not longe t'abyde.
>
> We han nought elles for to doon, y-wis.
> And Pandarus, now woltow trowen me?
> Have here my trouthe, I see hir! yond she is.
> Heve up thyn eyen, man! maystow not see?'
> Pandare answerde, 'nay, so mote I thee!
> Al wrong, by god; what seystow, man, wher art?
> That I see yond nis but a fare-cart.'

Criseyde herself, though like Pandarus she recedes, is also still there in the texture of the last book. Subsidiary to the behaviour of Troilus, but still of great relevance, is her behaviour in her altered situation and subject to the attentions and importunities of her foreign hero. Comedy persists in the last book substantially as this relationship between Diomede and Criseyde that supersedes the love between Troilus and Criseyde. The insinuations of Diomede and the equivocations of Criseyde are (ironically) an inferior and degraded version of the former love as that developed in the second book. Criseyde is answering Diomede:

> I am disposed bet, so mote I go,
> Un-to my deeth, to pleyne and maken wo,

> What I shal after doon, I can not seye,
> But trewely, as yet me list not pleye.
>
> My herte is now in tribulacioun,
> And ye in armes bisy, day by day,
> Here-after, whan ye wonnen han the toun . . .
>
> If that I sholde of any Greek han routhe,
> It sholde be your-selven, by my trouthe!
>
> I sey not therfore that I wol yow love,
> Ne I sey not nay, but in conclusioun,
> I mene wel, by god that sit above.

Criseyde's equivocations culminate in those of her final letter to Troilus, by which he at length understood that she

> N'as not so kinde as that hir oughte be.

Yet her faithlessness is recorded with all charitableness as forgivable human frailty. Fortune is more blamed than she. For the siege represents a dangerous and fatal division; and Troilus' fate is identified with that of Troy. Criseyde's fearfulness, from which her weakness partly arises, is the natural fearfulness of a defenceless woman between two hostile armies. Nor is it forgotten that Criseyde's human frailty is a counterpart not merely of her fearfulness but of her impressionable tender-heartedness.

7

The poem has compelled us to be aware of deficiencies in Troilus, Criseyde and Pandarus in relation to each other, and this is no negligible part of the poem's meaning. Yet the final judgment made by the poem is a judgment about humanity itself as represented by all three; it is that humanity is not self-sufficing. The final stanzas set the lovers and their story in their place in relation to the established mediaeval Christian values which Chaucer does not challenge; for the poem is no romantic glorification of passion. When Troilus' soul rising above the earth finally condemns

> The blinde lust, the which that may not laste

and profane love is described as 'worldly vanitee', the voice may not sound distinctively Chaucerian. Yet there is no ground whatever for supposing that these stanzas are a *moralitas* added perhaps by a Chaucer fallen into age, sickness and proximity to death as was, apparently, the 'retraccioun' added to the *Canterbury Tales*. If the voice is not distinctively Chaucerian, it is distinctively mediaeval, and makes explicit what has without doubt been implicit throughout the poem[1]—a portion of Chaucer's mediaeval gravity—that above the human love is to be set the love of God. Yet surely there is no more tenderly Chaucerian phrase in the whole of Chaucer than, in this context, 'O yonge fresshe folkes'.

> O yonge fresshe folkes, he or she,
> In which that love up groweth with your age,
> Repeyreth hoom from worldly vanitee,
> And of your herte up-casteth the visage
> To thilke god that after his image
> Yow made, and thinketh al nis but a fayre
> This world, that passeth sone as floures fayre.
>
> And loveth him, the which that right for love
> Upon a cros, our soules for to beye,
> First starf, and roos, and sit in hevene a-bove;

---

[1] In the second book already Criseyde, debating with herself whether or not to love, reflects:

> To what fyn is swich love, I can nat see,
> Or wher bicomth it, whan it is ago;
> There is no wight that woot, I trowe so,
> Wher it bycomth; lo, no wight on it sporneth;
> That erst was no-thing, in-to nought it torneth.

For he nil falsen no wight, dar I seye,
That wol his herte al hoolly on him leye.
And sin he best to love is, and most meke,
What nedeth feyned loves for to seke?

Troilus has 'leyde his herte al hoolly' on Criseyde instead of on Christ; that would appear to be the conclusion. Those of us who find this conclusion not in accordance with the great humane Chaucerian poem as a whole perhaps fall into the error of those who would ignore the context of Dante's Paolo and Francesca episode. For, as George Santayana has remarked, it is no accident that that apotheosis of types of passionate lovers absorbed in themselves and granted what they most of all desire and (the stern context implies) deserve, the torment of an ecstatic moment in each other's arms prolonged into eternity, is placed in the *Inferno*. It will be recognized that Chaucer's conclusion is therefore not discordant with that of Dante—the other serene, because clear, intelligence among the mediaeval poets.

THE LEGEND OF GOOD WOMEN

The *Legend of Good Women* has the distinction of being Chaucer's first collection of tales and the first poem in English in decasyllabic couplets, the characteristic metre of the *Canterbury Tales*. Yet, though in the chronology it rests in between *Troilus and Criseyde* and the *Canterbury Tales*, Chaucer's masterpieces, it does not engage, as they do, his powers as a great comic master. It is not substantially a poem of the human comedy, and is slighter; yet even here Chaucer's humour is occasionally felt as a genial presence, and, in one or two of the brief tales ('ensamples' of good womanhood) his dramatic power is occasionally immediate.

I

The Prologue to the *Legend of Good Women* is perhaps the loveliest, as it is certainly the maturest, of Chaucer's 'dream vision' poems in the tradition of *Le Roman de la Rose*. Chaucer's indebtedness here to the contemporary French poems of the Marguerite, the successors of *Le Roman de la Rose*, has been sufficiently elucidated by Livingston Lowes. The freshness of Chaucer's poem, as of eyes opening for the first time on the first morning of the world—

The fresshest sin the world was first bigonne—

is Chaucer's own and that of his English language just at this point in its growth. But the feeling for nature here, which so delighted nineteenth-century men-of-letters, is not, of course, a Wordsworthian feeling for nature. The daisy, the object of the poet's worship in the meadow on the May morning, is not simply itself; it is itself, but it is also something other than itself. The marguerite—

Swiche as men callen daysies in our toun

('our toun' being England as distinct from France)—had succeeded the rose in contemporary French poetry as a symbol. Who or what the daisy might be is gradually, reticently unfolded as the allegorical poem proceeds.

The waking worship of the daisy is succeeded by a dream vision in which the poet sees the God of Love approach across the meadow conducting a Queen who is clothed in green and crowned like a daisy; she *is* the daisy of his worship. The God and his Queen are evidently a courtly version or reminiscence of the May King and Queen of the village festivals. The speculation who or what the daisy is becomes now the speculation who or what this lady is. She and the god are accompanied by a multitude of women. The lines expressing the poet's wonder at their multitude seem to echo those lines in the *Inferno* that are echoed also in the lines—

83

A crowd flowed over London Bridge, so many,
I had not thought death had undone so many—

in Eliot's *Waste Land*. But Chaucer's countless multitude
of women are not damned (surely the contrast is humorously intended).

And trewe of love thise women were echoon.

The God of Love accuses Geoffrey Chaucer of heretical
discourtesy in having portrayed Criseyde as unfaithful to
her knight and in having translated the mocker, Jean de
Meung (presumably it is Jean's part of *Le Roman de la
Rose* that is here referred to). So the vision changes, in this
dramatic and comic scene, into a 'judgment of Geoffrey
Chaucer'. The lady in green has pity; she mercifully intercedes for the poet with the angry god, as Mary intercedes
for the sinner in Heaven.

The lady is not, of course, a religious figure as are
Beatrice or Matilda in the *Divina Comedia*; or the lady in
Ash Wednesday (who, though her role is different each
time she appears in the sequence, is always perhaps the
same lady, even in the third poem in which she is a distraction). She is clothed in the green of the May festival
(the colour is still more emphasized in the shorter version),
and otherwise unequivocally distinguished by her context
from Mary, Queen of Heaven, whose colour is blue—
'blue of larkspur, blue of Mary's colour'. She walks in an
earthly paradise which is yet not *the* Earthly Paradise of
the moral universe in which Matilda walks; it is literally a
meadow in a spring landscape, though she is seen in it in
a dream. Nevertheless, though not a religious figure, as
Beatrice or Matilda is, she is equally an allegorical figure.
She may, therefore, perhaps be more clearly understood
by pondering who Beatrice or Matilda is; her meaning,
like that of Beatrice or Matilda, is multiple, both literal
and symbolical. George Santayana elucidates this point in
the paragraphs on Beatrice in his chapter on Dante in
Three Philosophical Poets and in the chapter (from which

the following is quoted) on 'Platonic Love in Some Italian Poets' in *Poetry and Religion*.

'We need not, then, waste erudition in trying to prove whether Dante's Beatrice ... or any one else who has been the subject of the greater poetry of love, was a symbol or a reality. To poets and philosophers real things are themselves symbols. The child of seven whom Dante saw at the Florentine feast was, if you will, a reality. As such she is profoundly unimportant. ... It is intelligible that as time goes on that image, grown thus consciously symbolic, should become interchangeable with the abstract method of pursuing perfection—that Beatrice, that is, should become the same as sacred theology. Having recognized that she was to his childish fancy what the ideals of religion were to his mature imagination, Dante intentionally fused the two, as every poet intentionally fuses the general and the particular, the universal and the personal.'

The lady in green may, in the first instance, be a lady whom the poet was personally devoted to; she may well be intended to be associated with the Queen of England—Anne of Bohemia.[1] But if she is to be associated with the Queen, she is not (as some commentators have suggested) to be simply identified with the Queen, because at one point in the longer version of the poem (which is the version I am at present following) she herself speaks of the Queen of England as of another person.

---

[1] It is not inconceivable that the poem here is a reminiscence of a May Day pageant in which King Richard and Anne of Bohemia may have taken part. We may compare the description of Queen Guenevere going a-maying in Malory's *Morte Darthur* (Book XIX, Chapters I and II).

'How Queen Guenever rode on Maying with certain Knights of the Round Table and clad all in green.

'So it befell in the month of May, Queen Guenever called unto her knights of the Table Round; and she gave them warning that early upon the morrow she would ride on Maying into woods and fields beside Westminster. And I warn you that there be none of you but that he be well horsed, and that ye all be clothed in green, either in silk outher in cloth. ... So as the queen had Mayed and all her knights, all were bedashed with herbs, mosses and flowers, in the best manner and freshest.'

And whan this book is maad, yive hit the quene
On my behalfe, at Eltham, or at Shene.

When at length, at the end of the longer version, the lady
in green is named Alceste—the queen who died in place
of her husband, and the type of faithful womanhood—her
meaning is not, I think, felt to be expended by this identification of her with a 'historical' personage. We are told
that Alcestis was metamorphosed into a daisy (though
there appears to be no authority for this particular meta-
morphosis in the Classics).[1] The lady in green is the daisy
—or the daisy is she—and she is Alcestis; and she, who is
both the daisy and Alcestis and, perhaps, the Queen of
England, is herself a symbol; a symbol of the courtly ideal
of womanhood, the most exalted earthly (as distinguished
from heavenly) ideal—devotion to which made life courteous, gracious and gentle.

So far I have been keeping my eye on the longer version
of the Prologue. It has been the delight of pedants that
there are extant two versions of the Prologue, for it has
offered those who find nothing in poetry itself discussable,
and are sceptical that there can be such an activity as literary criticism, an opportunity to discuss the evidence as to
which is the earlier and which the later. Skeat originally
assumed that the longer was the later; Livingston Lowes
produces excellent (because partly literary critical) reasons
for concluding that, on the contrary, the longer is the
earlier. In fact it is evident (I will make bold to say) to any
one who simply views the two versions from no other
viewpoint but that of literary criticism—that is, who
attempts to see the two poems as what in fact in themselves
they are—which of the two is the revised version; the
shorter is so quite unmistakably the revised version that
one wonders what the long controversy and search for and
through extra-literary evidence has been all about.

The emotional overflow of the longer version has been

[1] We may recall (in relation to the seasonal theme) that Alcestis is
one of those who died and was restored again.

checked, the extravagance (as a more elderly and portlier Chaucer may himself have come to regard it) of the poet on his knees before the daisy, a whole day in that posture, has been eliminated; in general, the diffusion has been reduced, repetitions excised. But the shorter version is not simply the longer with passages missed out. There has been re-arrangement and clarification. A passage rather in the tone of the Wife of Bath's Prologue has even been added. The shorter version is, as a result, a soberer, more compact and more logical poem. Qualities have been sacrificed; some of the original freshness and spontaneity is gone; we would not wish that if a maturer Shakespeare had revised *Romeo and Juliet* we should have been deprived of the *Romeo and Juliet* we know. (The longer version of the Prologue may have continued the more popular, for it has come down on a dozen manuscripts, whereas the shorter has come down on only one.) The shorter is the more explicit, and it is hard to say whether this greater explicitness is totally a gain or a loss. We are less free to ponder who the lady in green might be because we are told almost at once that she is Alceste. The *ballade* which, in the longer version, is a personal expression of the courtly poet's devotion to his lady—

Hyde ye your beautes, Isoude and Eleyne,
My lady cometh, that al this may disteyne—

becomes the words of the song with which the ladies accompany the *carole* they dance in honour of Alceste; the shorter version is, as a whole, the more impersonal and objective. The longer may be the more poetical, but the shorter is the more complete poem; and the shorter has one image, introduced to herald the approach of the God of Love, which is perhaps the most imaginative of all the images in either poem.

Til at the laste a larke song above:
'I see', quod she, 'the mighty god of love!
Lo! yond he cometh, I see his winges sprede!'

In the shorter version the dream-vision begins—just before that image—with a remarkable expression of joy at the return of spring which is retained from the longer version. Spring was (we are told by the literary historians) a poetic convention. In the conventional poetry spring is, of course, conventional. But if Chaucer's joy here at the return of spring was a convention, then it was a convention in the sense that it was a way of feeling shared not merely with certain French poets but with the whole mediaeval folk. It would be a feeling that would not come to seem invalid to the poet growing older. Winter was a wretched enough time in actual experience for the mediaeval folk and the renewal of spring correspondingly welcome. The imaginative strength of the poetry comes from much deeper than poetic convention, from a response both traditional and personal, to the triumph of spring over winter immemorially celebrated in the annual dramatic rituals.

> Forgeten had the erthe his pore estat
> Of winter, that him naked made and mat,
> And with his swerd of cold so sore greved;
> Now hath the atempre sonne al that releved
> That naked was, and clad hit new agayn.
> The smale foules, of the seson fayn,
> That from the panter and the net ben scaped,
> Upon the fouler, that hem made a-whaped
> In winter, and distroyed had hir brood,
> In his despyt, hem thoughte hit did hem good
> To singe of him, and in hir song despyse
> The foule cherl that, for his covetyse,
> Had hem betrayed with his sophistrye.
> This was hir song—'the fouler we defye,
> And al his craft!' And somme songen clere
> Layes of love, that joye hit was to here,
> In worshipinge and praisinge of hir make.
> And, for the newe blisful somers sake,
> Upon the braunches ful of blosmes softe,
> In hir delyt, they turned hem ful ofte,

And songen, 'blessed be seynt Valentyn!
For on his day I chees yow to be myn,
Withouten repenting, myn herte swete!'
And therewith-al hir bekes gonnen mete,
Yelding honour and humble obeisaunces
To love, and diden hir other observaunces
That longeth unto love and to nature.

A familiar figure in the mediaeval countryside—for to
snare the little birds for food was a desperate necessity for
the mediaeval village communities in winter—the fowler
has here become a richly significant figure, as has Haukyn
the Waferman in *Piers Plowman* or Piers the Plowman
himself. He has acquired some of the value of Death and
the Devil.[1] He betrays the birds with his 'sophistrye'—
false, subtle arguments—as the Devil betrays the souls of
men with his nets and snares. The poet, with his mediaeval
sympathy for the creatures, can rejoice at their escape from
the winter and death, and can realize a correspondence
between their escape and that of the soul from the Devil.
With the spring also man himself escapes from the fowler's
necessity of snaring the birds, and himself escapes, as they
do, from winter and death and, at Easter, from the Fowler.

2

The legends themselves share with the versions of the
same tales in Gower's *Confessio Amantis* (which appears to
be exactly contemporary with the *Legend of Good Women*)
the distinction of being the earliest versions in English of
some of the most celebrated tales of the Graeco-Roman
world. Gower and Chaucer (the poetry of both has the
same social and cultural basis) evidently had the same
books in their libraries, and their ultimate source for most
of these tales appears to be Ovid. Chaucer may, in addi-

[1] The Fowler in Henryson's Fable of the *Swallow and the other Birds* is
explained in the *moralitas* as the Devil.

tion, have been indebted for the idea of his series of 'en-samples' of good women to Boccaccio's *De Claris Mulieribus*; and his heroines deserted (corresponding to Troilus deserted) appear to be indebted to the *Heroides* as much as to the *Metamorphoses*. The theme recurs in the *Canterbury Tales*; Dorigen by the seashore is, partly at least, a further variation of Ariadne by the seashore.

In the *Legend of Good Women* Chaucer has abandoned the short octo-syllabic line for the longer deca-syllabic line in rhymed couplets. He had become accustomed to move in the ampler line in the stanzas of *Troilus and Criseyde*. The lengthening of the line is in itself a small technical adjustment. But like many such small technical adjustments it had far-reaching consequences; it involved the fullest acceptance by Chaucer of a speech norm in place of the earlier song-and-dance (or 'carolling') norm. The short octo-syllabic line rhyming in couplets, as in the *Romaunt of the Rose*, tended to cause even conversational poetry to slip readily back into the earlier association with song— as the intricately metrical, assonantal poems of the troubadours had been associated with song. Poetry dominated too long by music tends to become conventional in a limiting sense, to be deprived of robustness and scope in handling life. The establishment of a conversational norm gave a chance to the steady and ordered Chaucerian observation and dramatization of life to develop. Though deca-syllabics in rhymed couplets were superseded in the sixteenth-century theatres by deca-syllabics without rhyme—the 'blank verse' developed in Elizabethan and Jacobean drama—deca-syllabics in rhymed couplets came in again, as a more strictly formalized mode in the poetry of Dryden, Pope, Johnson and Crabbe, in some ways the poetry of our most 'realistic' exposure of life. That is the measure of the centrality of Chaucer's choice of this metre for the greater part of the *Canterbury Tales*; it is first tried out in the *Legend of Good Women*.

The first of the 'good women' is Cleopatra, faithful unto death, now one of the company of Love's martyrs or

Cupid's saints. She is a courtly mediaeval lady, 'fair as is the rose in May', and she loves her knight, Antony, for his 'chivalrye' and his 'gentilesse'. Whatever Chaucer's sources and whatever the associations we bring from our own reading the poetic world of the *Legend of Good Women* is an independent world, complete in itself, and should be accepted as what in itself it is.

The tale of Pyramus and Thisbe is the first of the tales from Ovid. But it has an entirety of innocence as told by Chaucer which is wholly different from the Augustan sophistication of Ovid.

> And every day this wal they wolde threte,
> And wisshe to god, that it were doun y-bete.
> Thus wolde they seyn—'allas! thou wikked wal ...'

The melancholy idyll of the garden-wall, cruel obstruction between the childlike lovers, contrasts with, yet belongs to the same world of primary passion as the brutality of their deaths in the tragic wood.

> And at the laste her love than hath she founde
> Beting with his heles on the grounde,
> Al blody, and therwith-al a-bak she sterte,
> And lyke the wawes quappe gan her herte.

The source of the legend of Dido again appears to have been more Ovid than Virgil. Dido and Aeneas going hunting is a glowing mediaeval tapestry scene that has gained a Chaucerian human depth, particularly from the couplet.

> And she is fair, as is the brighte morwe,
> That heleth seke folk of nightes sorwe ...

and, in Chaucer, even an element of humour hovers in the vicinity of the dreadful storm scene on the same celebrated hunting occasion, perceptible in the mock-innocence of

> She fledde her-self into a litel cave,
> And with her wente this Eneas al-so;

91

> I noot with hem if ther wente any mo;
> The autour maketh of hit no mencioun.

Humour is again present as an element in the reverberating denunciation of that 'false fox', Jason, which introduces the legends of his victims, Hypsipyle and Medea. This presence of humour in the legends implies a criticism, not of Ovid, but of the mediaeval conventionalized idealism in terms of which Ovid had been reinterpreted; it clears the way for real human feeling. In the legend of Medea, the theme of which is the desertion of Medea by Jason, human feeling is delicately rendered because delicately understood.

> 'Why lyked me thy yelow heer to see
> More then the boundes of myn honestee . . .'

But the two legends in which Chaucer's knowledge of the heart is most fully dramatized are the legends of Lucretia and Ariadne. In the former, Tarquin and his officers, bored with camp life, discuss their wives and ride to Rome to observe them. The wifely Lucretia, in an idyllic domestic scene while her husband is (supposedly) absent at the wars, fulfils her husband's praises; Tarquin is unable afterwards to get her image out of his mind.

> Th' image of her recording alwey newe;
> 'Thus lay her heer, and thus fresh was her hewe;
> Thus sat, thus spak, thus span; this was her chere,
> Thus fair she was, and this was her manere.'
> All this conceit his herte hath now y-take.
> And, as the see, with tempest al to-shake,
> That, after whan the storm is al ago,
> Yet wol the water quappe a day or two,
> Right so, thogh that her forme wer absent,
> The plesaunce of her forme was present.

But the masterpiece of dramatic presentation in the legends is that of Ariadne deserted. It is more than a most spectacular visualization—and it is a spectacular visualization; it is a scene, a person and an action, dramatically presented. The presentation has gained an additional dimension from the realization of the sense of loss at the heart of Ariadne's distraction, and the consequent tact, as well as sympathetic accuracy, with which distracted human behaviour is rendered.

> Right in the dawening awaketh she,
> And gropeth in the bedde, and fond right noght.
> 'Allas!' quod she, 'that ever I was wroght!
> I am betrayed!' and her heer to-rente,
> And to the stronde bar-fot faste she wente,
> And cryed, 'Theseus! myn herte swete!
> Wher be ye, that I may nat with yow mete,
> And mighte thus with bestes been y-slain?'
> The holwe rokkes answerde her again;
> No man she saw, and yit shyned the mone,
> And hye upon a rokke she wente sone,
> And saw his barge sailing in the see.
> Cold wex her herte, and right thus seide she.
> 'Meker than ye finde I the bestes wilde!'

That Ovid counted, in addition to the French and Italians, in the evolution of Chaucer's sensibility and art there seems no reason to doubt; the lines

> And cryed, 'Theseus! myn herte swete . . .
> The holwe rokkes answerde her again

though more simply human are sufficiently close to the central effect of

> Interea toto clamanti litore 'Theseu!'
> Reddebant nomen concava saxa tuum,
> Et quotiens ego te, totiens locus ipse vocabat.

It is the Chaucer of some of the *Canterbury Tales* we recognize already in these scenes. The legends of Philomela and Phyllis (again from Ovid) are the last completed legends. The tragic legend of Phyllis ends incongruously with an outbreak of humour—

Be war, ye women, of your sotil fo,
Sin yit this day men may ensample see;
And trusteth, as in love, no man but me.[1]

—an outbreak that suggests that the Chaucer of the *Canterbury Tales* (as by this time he was in fact becoming) was unable to pursue solemnly to the bitter end a series of lamentable tragedies on the single theme of faithful or deserted women. The poem breaks off in the middle of the next legend.

[1] 'me' i.e. Geoffrey Chaucer.

94

PART TWO

THE CANTERBURY TALES

THE CANTERBURY TALES

I

The *Canterbury Tales* is the completion of Chaucer's poetry; it was his work in the last decade of the fourteenth century and of his life. One or two of the tales are, or appear to be, early. But the great Prologue, the interludes between the tales and the majority of the tales are unmistakably the creation of Chaucer's fullest maturity.

In relation to the planned whole, the work is a succession of fragments. The position of the great Prologue is, of course, not in doubt. Nor is there any doubt that the first tale was intended to be the Knight's, and that it was to be succeeded by the Miller's, the Reve's and the Cook's. After this first group there is a break. The *Canterbury Tales* consists of several such groups which had evidently not been placed in any final order when Chaucer died. Yet the impression the great poem leaves upon the mind is anything but that of a fragmentary work; it is a poem complete in itself as an impression of the diversity and plenitude of human life—'God's plenty'.

In the *Canterbury Tales* narrative art is at the point of becoming drama. The poem is the culmination of Chaucer's dramatic-poetic development of English speech; and something unaccountably *new* in mediaeval literature. The *personae* are first presented in the great Prologue with a vividness not attained before in English, even by Chaucer, and seldom since. Thereafter, in the comic interludes between the tales, they begin to move and talk and act. The Wife of Bath's preamble—which is twice the length of her tale—is the Wife herself talking, enacting scenes and dialogues between herself and her several husbands, dramatizing her private life in front of an audience; her tale

G   97

itself is the Wife continuing to talk. The Pardoner's Prologue and Tale are another character's self-dramatization. The *Canterbury Tales* thus presents a company of distinct and individual people talking; the tales are a part of themselves and their talk. The interest is not simply in the tale —vivid as it nearly always is in itself—but, at the same time, in the teller and in the tale as characteristic of the teller. The variety of the tales reproduces and fulfils the initial human variety. Each tale dramatically projects a distinct person. It is hard for us to credit (after it has happened) how new were the possibilities realized for the first time in the *Canterbury Tales*; the poem is the beginning of English dramatic and fictional literature as a whole. The 'so seemingly unstudied'[1] technical accomplishment of the great Prologue, the comic interludes and the maturest tales is the fulfilment of a process of experiment and exploration which was more than technical; it is an aspect of the depth and maturity of Chaucer's daringly achieved vision of human life.

The *Canterbury Tales* is the Human Comedy of the Middle Ages. Dante's *Divine Comedy* is a rationally ordered vision of the *moral* universe. In the *Inferno* the categories of evil, as Dante had particularly experienced and identified these in his Italy, are each apprehended and placed according to its degree. By way of the *Purgatorio* the ascent is made through the intervening planes of being, to the climax of the *Paradiso*. Dante thus, in a single vision, comprehends man in the multiplicity of his relationship to God—through each of the spheres of moral being, from states of perdition (or utter deprivation of God) to the higher and highest states of beatitude (or contemplative love of God). In the *Canterbury Tales* the object of the poet's contemplation is the human order as in itself it is, having its place in a divinely established natural order; it is presented as immediately as it presented itself to Chaucer's alert perception in his contemporary England. The procession of Chaucer's Canterbury pilgrims is the pro-

[1] Coleridge.

98

cession of the Human Comedy. It is *Le Pelèrinage de la Vie Humaine* (as Blake recognized, it has both a timeless and a temporal aspect. 'They are the physiognomies and lineaments of universal human life.')

> This world nis but a thurghfare ful of wo,
> And we ben pilgrimes, passinge to and fro.
>
> (Knight's Tale)

But the tone of Chaucer's company of English folk is as a whole one of jollity; and, scandalously careless in relation to eternity as several of the company appear to be, this jollity accords with the tone of grateful acceptance of life which is the tone of the *Canterbury Tales* as a whole. The *personae* of the comedy are so vivid that we feel them (as Dryden did) to be our immediate contemporaries and are apt to miss the depth of difference of their background; yet it is that unfamiliar depth which lends the vivid comedy its richer significance. A way of life, a whole phase of civilization different in many respects from our own— though our own has evolved from it—goes to the composing of that Chaucerian depth. The human comedy of the *Canterbury Tales* moves within an apprehension of an all-inclusive divine harmony. There is no mitigation of the evil in the Canterbury pilgrims nor in the characters of their tales; indeed, the rogues and scoundrels have been remarked to predominate in the *Canterbury Tales*. Yet the divine order—in relation to which we are all judged—is not felt to be disturbed, and the contemplation of even the 'evil' characters is correspondingly steady. Life in its totality—both 'good' and 'evil'—is accepted as exactly what it is observed to be.

2

THE PROLOGUE

The opening of the *Canterbury Tales* implies what the tales will unfold and variously illustrate. It is, appropriately, a superb expression of a sense of harmony between man and nature. The creative uprush of new life from the roots in spring is profoundly and accurately experienced and realized in poetry that is liberated from conventional diction.

> Whan that Aprille with his shoures sote
> The droghte of Marche hath perced to the rote,
> And bathed every veyne in swich licour,
> Of which vertu engendred is the flour;
> Whan Zephirus eek with his swete breeth
> Inspired hath in every holt and heeth
> The tendre croppes, and the yonge sonne
> Hath in the Ram his halfe cours y-ronne,
> And smale fowles maken melodye,
> That slepen al the night with open yë,
> (So priketh hem nature in hir corages):
> Than longen folk to goon on pilgrimages . . .

The wave of impulse which causes the birds to mate, as well as the plants to grow, is shared by the human folk.

> Than longen folk to goon on pilgrimages.

The comment is an instance of Chaucer's humour, the way in which he controls his first flow of impulse and a too easy acceptance of it. The desire to go on pilgrimages is, after all, he implies not without irony, something like the migrating impulse in birds. But its end is worship.

Thus the human order is nevertheless realized as having its place in Nature. A criterion of human 'naturalness' is thus implied right at the beginning of the great poem. The spring landscape across which the human procession passes is not merely a decorative background; it *is* the divinely established[1] natural order in relation to which the human comedy is to be contemplated and judged.

It is instructive, if we wish to understand ourselves, to compare this opening to the *Canterbury Tales* with the opening to the *Waste Land*.

[1] *Kynd* is explicitly identified with God in *Piers Plowman*. Passus IX.

April is the cruellest month, breeding
Lilacs out of the dead land, mixing
Memory and desire, stirring
Dull roots with spring rain.
Winter kept us warm, covering
Earth in forgetful snow, feeding
A little life with dried tubers.
Summer surprised us, coming over the Starnbergersee
With a shower of rain; we stopped in the colonnade,
And went on in sunlight, into the Hofgarten,
And drank coffee, and talked for an hour.

A comparison ought to begin from an acknowledgment
that both openings are authentic poetry. The difference
that emerges between them is the difference between two
phases of civilization. The modern poem involves a consciousness of disharmony between man and nature, a dis-
organization and dislocation of life. Something has gone
wrong with the orderly relationship between man and
nature which is Chaucer's joyous starting-point.

And drank coffee, and talked for an hour.

Than longen folk to goon on pilgrimages.

The line in the modern poem conveys the aimlessness of
rootless lives which no longer appear to themselves to have
a social or other function. Not that there is any inertness
in the rhythm of the modern passage as a whole; on the
contrary, it expresses, in its strong positive rhythm, a positive dissatisfaction with the negative spiritual condition
which it consciously presents. Nevertheless, the contrast
with the vital joyous springing rhythm of the opening of
the *Canterbury Tales* is inescapable.[1]

---

[1] This comparison should be extended to the superb opening movements
of *East Coker* and *Little Gidding*.

> There is no earth smell
> Or smell of living thing. This is the spring time
> But not in time's covenant. Now the hedgerow

As if issuing from this harmony between the natural and the human orders, the characters who are to talk and act and tell the tales are presented.

'What the creator of character needs is not so much knowledge of motives as keen sensibility; the dramatist need not understand people; but he must be exceptionally aware of them.' (T. S. Eliot)

The Prologue is the outcome of an exceptional awareness of people, not of a mass, but of distinct persons who, entering in a succession, combine into an impression of a people, the English people; they constitute temporarily a company. This small community seems, somehow, to imply the *whole* of Chaucer's contemporary English community. Though not numerous—

> Wel nyne and twenty in a companye
> Of sondry folk . . .

—the impression (such is their Chaucerian diversity) is of a plentiful folk,

> . . . born
> Out of the mouth of Plenty's horn[1]

> Is blanched for an hour with transitory blossom
> Of snow, a bloom more sudden
> Than that of summer, neither budding nor fading,
> Not in the scheme of generation.
> Where is the summer, the unimaginable
> Zero summer?

These movements, nevertheless, imply a rejection of 'Nature' for 'Eternity'. The *Waste Land* remains an integral part of Eliot's poetry and, therefore, of the modern consciousness. In *The Rainbow* we start from a traditional rural life in unison with the natural rhythms but move out towards the larger intelligent life. 'We have lost . . . our delight in the whole man—blood, imagination, intellect, running together,' said Yeats. In the images at the conclusion of his poem, *Among School Children*, he attains for a moment a triumphant apprehension of such a harmony.

> O chestnut tree, great rooted blossomer,
> Are you the leaf, the blossom or the bole?
> O body swayed to music, O brightening glance,
> How can we know the dancer from the dance?

[1] Yeats: *A Prayer for my Daughter*.

who establish among themselves, without external compulsion, a community.

The Knight, the Squire and their attendant Yeoman evidently form a group, a distinct element in this community. The rather faded, crusading Knight is felt as already passing into the past, rememberable for an inner beauty of life beneath his battered exterior expressed in the tenderly nostalgic line

> He was a verray parfit gentil knight.

An inner beauty of life is felt as shared by several among the least externally distinct figures in the procession, the Knight, the Poor Parson and his brother the Plowman—

> Livinge in pees and parfit charitee.

It cannot be accidental that the Knight has this quality in common with the Plowman; they are blood-brothers in Christ.

The immediate contrast to the ageing Knight is his son, the young Squire, the eternal young bachelor (Sir Mirthe and Youthe), an extravagant spring-like figure—the new generation—but truly accomplished and courtly.

> Embrouded was he, as it were a mede
> Al ful of fresshe floures, whyte and rede.
> Singinge he was, or floytinge, al the day;
> He was as fresh as is the month of May.

The external fadedness of the Knight is emphasized by this sharp contrast with the gay extravagance of the young Squire and with the spectacular Robin-Hood-like apparition of the Yeoman who is, underneath, simply a solid English countryman.

> A not-heed hadde he, with a broun visage.

But Chaucer's most serious 'criticism of life' in the Prologue is implied in his presentation of the ecclesiastics. The art is in seeing exactly what each is in relation to what each ought to be; an art of exact contemplation but not in a void. That the criticism is implied itself implies an audience which shared the same social and moral standards as the poet. The art is as much in what is left unsaid as in what is said; and what is said consists in the simple juxtaposition of statements which it is left to the audience to know how to relate.[1] How alert, intelligent and civilized Chaucer's audience must have been to understand exactly what is left unsaid, to see the point of the irony! Could any such audience be assembled in any theatre to-day, or even as a select company in a private house?

It is in the presentation of the Prioresse that the most delicately poised irony is apprehensible.

> That of hir smyling was ful simple and coy;
> Hir gretteste ooth was but by sëynt Loy;
> And she was cleped madam Eglentyne.
> Ful wel she song the service divyne,
> Entuned in hir nose ful semely.

Her 'smyling ful simple and coy' already suggests a young girl in the presence of young men rather than a prioress. The name Eglentyne, a wild rose, is also a little unexpected as a name for a prioress (even against a spring background) though, as it turns out, not entirely inappropriate for this Prioresse. Whether or not her singing is to be regarded rather as a social accomplishment or the devout performance of a religious office we may as yet be unable to conclude; but, whichever way we regard it, the insistence on the image 'in hir nose' gently discomposes the propriety, upsets the solemnity of the decorum, the 'seme-lihede'.

> At mete wel y-taught was she with-alle;
> She leet no morsel from hir lippes falle,
> Ne wette hir fingres in hir sauce depe.
> Wel coude she carie a morsel, and wel kepe,
> That no drope ne fille up-on hir brest.

[1] The unexpectedness of these juxtapositions is often of the essence of the wit.

In curteisye was set ful muche hir lest.
Hir over lippe wyped she so clene,
That in hir coppe was no ferthing sene
Of grece, whan she dronken hadde hir draughte.
Ful semely after hir mete she raughte . . .

Her table manners not only show that she has been gen-
teelly brought up, that she is a lady, but are somewhat
excessively important, their dainty ritual and nicety over-
elaborated, in one dedicated after all to the rigour of the
monastic life.

And ful plesaunt, and amiable of port,
And peyned hir to countrefete chere
Of court, and been estatlich of manere,
And to ben holden digne of reverence.

Her anxiety (for she is somewhat would-be) to 'ben holden
digne of reverence' by affectation of courtly manners
rather than by holiness of life confirms the underlying note
of worldly vanity. We catch a fleeting glimpse of the
courtly lady of the Rose under the nun's dress of our delightful madame Eglentyne. Her way of life conforms less
to the monastic ideal than to the ideal of courtly manners.
The two ideals might, perhaps, be harmonized. But the
propriety of 'curteisye' as the first and foremost ideal for a
prioress may be doubted. The irony is in the doubt.

But, for to speken of hir conscience,
She was so charitable and so pitous,
She wolde wepe, if that she sawe a mous
Caught in a trappe, if it were deed or bledde.
Of smale houndes had she, that she fedde
With rosted flesh, or milk and wastelbreed.
But sore weep she if oon of hem were deed,
Or if men smoot it with a yerde smerte:
And al was conscience and tendre herte.

'Conscience' does not (whatever the editors may tell us)
correspond to Jane Austen's 'sensibility'. Religion had al-

ready something more active to do with the word (as we can see from its use in Langland). Nevertheless, what is peculiar about this Prioresse's 'conscience' is that it is not strictly, as we should expect in a prioress, a conscious feeling guided by religion but an effusion of tender sympathies that is sentimental because neither directed towards the most appropriate objects nor proportionate to its objects. The charity and pity of a prioress might more appropriately have been expended on the poor, the hungry, the sick and the suffering than on mice and small dogs. Charity and pity, excellent in a prioress if directed where the need is the greatest, are lavished on pet dogs fed daintily and expensively. The social historians tell us that nuns were, strictly speaking, forbidden to keep pet dogs. It seems improbable that Chaucer and his audience should have been conscious of this prohibition and the Prioresse not (it is not in her character to be consciously rebellious). I therefore hesitate to see in that the point of the irony.

> Ful semely hir wimpel pinched was;
> Hir nose tretys; hir eyen greye as glas;
> Hir mouth ful smal, and there-to softe and reed;
> But sikerly she hadde a fair forheed;
> It was almost a spanne brood, I trowe;
> For, hardily, she was nat undergrowe.
> Ful fetis was hir cloke, as I was war.
> Of smal coral aboute hir arm she bar
> A peire of bedes, gauded al with grene;
> And there-on heng a broche of gold ful shene,
> On which ther was first write a crowned A,
> And after, Amor vincit omnia.

The distinct visualization presents an elegant lady rather than a nun. The mouth (which is the mouth of one who might appropriately be called Sweet-Briar) makes an immediate contrast with the exposed broad forehead. (Again the social historians make the point, which it is again not certain is the point here, that nuns were forbidden to expose the forehead). The gradually evolved ambiguity in this presentation of the Prioresse culminates in the final ambiguity of *Amor Vincit Omnia*. *Amor* might be expected in the case of a prioress to mean only one thing, *Amor Dei*. But this Prioresse is just sufficiently a lady of the world, and a sentimentalist, for a doubt to exist as to whether it is the divine love or the profane courtly love sentiment that is intended. That doubt, if it exists (and in the context it surely does exist), has to be taken account of as an aspect of the character. The irony is in this ambiguity within the character itself; and also as the character is seen, with its slight affectation, in relation to the spring season and to nature.

The irony implied in the presentation of the Monk depends on a less ambiguous contrast between his grosser worldliness and his monastic profession. This hunting Monk is one of those lords of creation who ride across all the rules; his bridle's profane sound rivals the chapel bell.

> An out-rydere, that loved venerye;
> A manly man, to been an abbot able.
> Ful many a deyntee hors hadde he in stable:
> And, whan he rood, men mighte his brydel here
> Ginglen in a whistling wind as clere,
> And eek as loude as dooth the chapel belle
> Ther as this lord was keper of the celle.

Again the social historians tell us that hunting—certainly pride in horses and dogs—was against the monastic rule. But the quality of this lordly Monk's 'manliness' is very soon defined as being incompatible not only with the rules but with any discipline of mind and body.

> The reule of seint Maure or of seint Beneit,
> By-cause that it was old and som-del streit,
> This ilke monk leet olde thinges pace,
> And held after the newe world the space.

This particular kind of summary rejection of the past is simply a pre-condition to his doing as he pleases. The colloquialisms with which he dismisses the texts—

> He yaf nat of that text a pulled hen . . .
>
> But thilke text held he nat worth an oistre . . .

express the gusto and contemptuous horse-sense of the
sensual man (as in the *fabliaux*) in opposition to the scholar
and the saint with whom a monk ought nevertheless to
have taken his stand. Contempt for the incapacities of
unworldly monks, their helplessness in the world outside
the cloister (which becomes one of the implications in this
context of

> Ne that a monk, whan he is cloisterlees,
> Is lykned til a fish that is waterlees)

is understandable, perhaps, as an attitude of the labouring
and unlettered peasant folk. But it is scarcely excusable in
one who is himself a monk, because his boasted freedom
from monkish incapacities implies that he should not have
been a monk at all. Whether or not 'his opinioun was good'
(in the context the irony is surely unmistakable) it is
scarcely the opinion appropriate to one who has taken the
monastic vows. The argument which follows purports to
sustain that 'And I seyde, his opinioun was good', but
really undermines it. When it is examined it turns out to
be no argument at all.

> And I seyde, his opinioun was good.
> What sholde he studie, and make himselven wood,
> Upon a book in cloistre alwey to poure,
> Or swinken with his handes, and laboure,
> As Austin bit? How shal the world be served?

The Monk's vocation was not to serve 'the world' but to
serve God. Even if the world is taken here in the sense of
'mankind', it can no more be served than can God by
doing no work, manual or other. 'Austin bit' the monk
also 'swinken with his handes and laboure' like the peasant; and that command is not really dismissed at all, as is
pretended, by that perfectly bogus 'How shal the world

be served'. There is in fact no opposition here between the studious bookish man, the learned clerk, and the manual labourer, the peasant or craftsman. The real opposition is between the studious disciplined man (which this Monk is not) and the sensual worldly man (which this Monk is) who wastes his energies in sensual pleasure and continual sport. To read the passage as expressing Chaucer's moral approval of the Monk is complacently to identify Chaucer and oneself with the sensual man. Chaucer no doubt delightedly appreciates the Monk as a fine specimen, a rich *ensample*, but that he does not approve of him the irony most clearly indicates.

> Grehoundes he hadde, as swifte as fowel in flight;
> Of priking and of hunting for the hare
> Was all his lust, for no cost wolde he spare.

This is a grosser waste and misdirection of energy than the Prioresse's excess of tenderness for mice and pampering of 'smale houndes'. Unlike the Prioresse's *Amor vincit omnia*, the signification of the love-knot at the end of the gold pin which fastens the Monk's hood under his chin is not in doubt. The distinct visualization shows us a well cared for, over-indulged, pampered body.

> His heed was balled, that shoon as any glas,
> And eek his face, as he had been anoint.
> He was a lord ful fat and in good point;
> His eyen stepe, and rollinge in his heed,
> That stemed as a forneys of a leed;
> His botes souple, his hors in greet estat.

'As he had been anoint' contains within itself a contrast between the holy oil and his greasy fatness; 'in good point', as might be said of a horse or dog, implies his animality. The irony is concentrated in the final ambiguity—

> Now certeinly he was a fair prelat

109

—which confirms the irony right at the beginning—

> A manly man, to been an abbot able.

In what sense is he 'a fair prelat'?

> Now certeinly he was a fair prelat;
> He was nat pale as a for-pyned goost.
> A fat swan loved he best of any roost.

This lover of good feeding and good hunting is 'fair' in the worldly, the corporal, not spiritual sense.

The Friar, again seen simply as what and for what he is (another rich *ensample*) makes a broader implied contrast with what he ought to be. The traditional themes of covetousness and abuse of confession, the more outrageous in one vowed to celibacy, form the basic moral pattern of the 'character'.

> Ful wel biloved and famulier was he
> With frankeleyns over-al in his contree,
> And eek with worthy wommen of the toun:
> For he had power of confessioun,
> As seyde him-self, more than a curat,
> For of his ordre he was licentiat.
> Ful swetely herde he confessioun,
> And plesaunt was his absolucioun;
> He was an esy man to yeve penaunce
> Ther as he wiste to han a good pitaunce;
> For unto a povre ordre for to yive
> Is signe that a man is wel y-shrive.
> For if he yaf, he dorste make avaunt,
> He wiste that a man was repentaunt.
> For many a man so hard is of his herte,
> He may nat wepe al-thogh him sore smerte,
> Therfore, in stede of weping and preyeres,
> Men moot yeve silver to the povre freres.

Yet the quietude of the amused contemplation, undistorted by exasperation with human delinquency or by exertion of the will to abuse or chastise, is such that even here 'satire' seems not to be the right word.

> His tipet was ay farsed ful of knyves
> And pinnes, for to yeven faire wyves.

The ribald *fabliau* attitude to monks and friars as all, simply as such, suspect has been resolved into a completer wisdom and subtler art.

> His nekke whyt was as the flour-de-lys;
> Ther-to he strong was as a champioun.

Besides suggesting, in implied contrast with the tanned neck of a labouring peasant, the delicate whiteness of the neck of the very able-bodied Friar (the contrast of the two lines is characteristic), the simile of the fleur-de-lys introduces an almost burlesque effect by which the spirit is lightened from the oppressive triumph of the jolly holidaying scoundrel. For the Friar, of course, rides triumphantly in the succession of the sins of the flesh and of avarice. His human relationships are determined not by his religious obligations, which would direct him to 'lazars' and 'beggesteres', but, like those of Fals-semblant, by his gluttony.

> He knew the tavernes wel in every toun,
> And everich hostiler and tappestere
> Bet than a lazar or a beggestere;
> For un-to swich a worthy man as he
> Acorded nat, as by his facultee,
> To have with seke lazars aqueyntaunce.
> It is nat honest, it may nat avaunce
> For to delen with no swich poraille,
> But al with riche and sellers of vitaille.

His distinction as a member of a religious order is that

> He was the beste beggere in his hous; . . .
> For thogh a widwe hadde noght a sho . . .
> Yet wolde he have a ferthing, er he wente.

His predatory covetousness exploits the charity of those who are themselves in direst need of charity. Thus, when at the end, we are presented in that excellent simile of the bell with his round, prosperous, blown-up image, we are already perfectly aware of its immoral basis.

> For there he was nat lyk a cloisterer,
> With a thredbar cope, as is a povre scoler,
> But he was lyk a maister or a pope.
> Of double worsted was his semi-cope,
> That rounded as a belle out of the presse.
> Somewhat he lipsed, for his wantownesse.

There ensues a succession of secular figures, *ensamples* of characters engaged in diverse secular occupations, mostly of the new 'middle class' which was emerging in the towns of Chaucer's England. Each is vividly distinct from the other and further contributes to the amassing of an impression of a rich diversity of human folk. The Seven Deadly Sins (which had passed into literature through the vernacular sermons) continue to nourish the roots of the subtle individual characterization; thus Gluttony underlies the Frankeleyn, Avarice the Doctour of Phisyk.

There is no space here to appreciate each of these vivid, and complex, figures as each deserves. Keeping up appearances is the keynote of the Marchant—

> A Marchant was ther with a forked berd,
> In mottelee, and hye on horse he sat,
> Up-on his heed a Flaundrish bever hat . . .
> His resons he spak ful solempnely,
> Souninge alway th'encrees of his winning.

The monotony of the Marchant's conversation is wonderfully conveyed in that last line. There is a grave discrepancy between the appearance he keeps up and what lies behind the appearance.

> Ther wiste no wight that he was in dette.

The Man of Lawe, too, keeps up an elaborate pretence.

> No-wher so bisy a man as he ther nas,
> And yet he semed bisier than he was.

He is busy about many vain things; like the Marchant, he seems wiser than he is.

> He semed swich, his wordes weren so wyse.

His accumulated legal learning has only a cash value for him. In short, the Marchant and the Man of Lawe are both worldly men in contrast to the Clerk of Oxenford, the unworldly scholar of all time.

The Frankeleyn is one of the most vivid of the secular figures.

> Whyt was his berd, as is the dayesye.
> Of his complexioun he was sangwyn.

Ruddiness of colour is, of course, a secondary implication of 'sangwyn complexioun'; yet it seems likely that the visual impression—ruddy 'complexion' in the modern sense—is an immediately relevant one here in contrast to the white beard.

> Wel loved he by the morwe a sop in wyn.
> To liven in delyt was ever his wone,
> For he was Epicurus owne sone,
> That heeld opinioun, that pleyn delyt
> Was verraily felicitee parfyt.

The contrast between 'pleyn delyt' and 'felicitee parfyt' is evidently intended to be sharp, and is the key to the Frankeleyn's confusion, arising from his gluttony, as to what constitutes 'felicitee parfyt' and the ends of living. Nevertheless, he keeps open house as a bountiful and generous host.

> Seint Julian he was in his contree.

His house holds the abundant prodigality of nature.

> A bettre envyned man was no-wher noon.

> With-oute bake mete was never his hous,
> Of fish and flesh, and that so plentevous,
> It snewed in his hous of mete and drinke.

The images throughout ('whyt as morne milk') present a robust *ensample* of a self-indulgent country gentleman or land-owner in an environment of natural plenty.

The group of Guildsmen are, in contrast, prospering townsmen.

> Wel semed ech of hem a fair burgeys,
> To sitten in a yeldhalle on a deys.
> Everich, for the wisdom that he can,
> Was shaply for to been an alderman.
> For catel hadde they y-nogh and rente,
> And eek hir wyves wolde it wel assente;
> And elles certein were they to blame.
> It is ful fair to been y-clept 'ma dame',
> And goon to vigilyës al bifore,
> And have a mantel royalliche y-bore.

There is clearly an affinity between these wives and the Wife of Bath; they are just as sinfully proud.

> And elles certein were they to blame.

The phrase is of the same order as

> And I seyde, his opinioun was good.

The Cook significantly attends this group, a real London cook. The Shipman represents, among these townsmen and landsmen, another of the traditional occupations of the English people.

> With many a tempest hadde his berd been shake.

He is a rude half-civilized fellow.

> Of nyce conscience took he no keep.

But the learned and proficient Doctour of Phisyk is just

114

as conscienceless. The key-note of this somewhat sinister figure is Avarice.

> Ful redy hadde he his apothecaries,
> To sende him drogges and his letuaries,
> For ech of hem made other for to winne;
> Hir frendschipe nas nat newe to biginne . . .
> His studie was but litel on the bible.
> In sangwin and in pers he clad was al,
> Lyned with taffata and with sendal;
> And yet he was but esy of dispence;
> He kepte that he wan in pestilence.
> For gold in phisik is a cordial,
> Therfore he loved gold in special.

The most vivid of all the secular figures is the Wife of Bath. The critical irony accompanying her presentation depends again on the contrast, in relation to her, between formal religious observance and profane impulse. She is neither more nor less a profane figure than are the ecclesiastics of the company, in their differing degrees of delicacy or indelicacy, the Prioresse, the Monk, the Friar.

> In al the parisshe wyf ne was ther noon
> That to th'offring bifore hir sholde goon;
> And if ther dide, certeyn, so wrooth was she,
> That she was out of alle charitee.

'Charitee' is the key word of the irony here, as 'conscience' is at one point in the presentation of the Prioresse; it reminds us of the obligation of Christian neighbourliness which she is forgetful of at a rather unexpected time and place. Her uncharitableness, in church, proceeds from Pride which at this point, in her own unique way, she typifies. She must go before, in that respect have the 'maistrye'; and it is especially on a Sunday of all days that her vanity flares out, is flaunted in flamboyant costume.

> Hir coverchiefs ful fyne were of ground;
> I dorste swere they weyeden ten pound

That on a Sonday were upon hir heed.
Hir hosen weren of fyn scarlet reed,
Ful streite y-teyd, and shoos ful moiste and newe.

Within the Comedy of the Sins (later, that of the Humours, Jonsonian Comedy) there is here perceptible an element also of social comedy. The Wife is a new social type, an exuberant *ensample* of the newly opulent, ostentatious cloth-making bourgeoisie—though her costume is amusingly not *quite* the height of fashion. (The social historians inform us that such head-dress was no longer the fashion among the ladies of the Court.) But, of course, the Wife of Bath is neither merely a type of an emergent class nor is she one of those terrible Langlandian caricatures, the Deadly Sins. As a fully individual, whole person of the same Shakespearian order as Falstaff, she has rich human value. In spite of (or even with the more force because of) her loud dress and manner, she is realized as a humanly attractive as well as a dazzling figure, a gay, talkative, formidable, dominating person.

Bold was hir face, and fair, and reed of hewe.
She was a worthy womman al hir lyve,
Housbondes at chirche-dore she hadde fyve,
Withouten other companye in youthe.

Parallel with her many amorous adventures are her many far pilgrimages; she is restless, adventurous, curious.

She coude much of wandring by the weye.

The phrase is very likely subtler than it at first seems, if as is nearly certain it contains an allusion to the errant soul.

Gat-tothed was she, soothly for to seye.
Up-on an amblere easily she sat,
Y-wimpled wel, and on hir heed an hat
As brood as is a bokeler or a targe;
A foot-mantel aboute hir hipes large,
And on hir feet a paire of spores sharpe.
In felawschip wel coude she laughe and carpe.

> Of remedyes of love she knew perchaunce,
> For she coude of that art the olde daunce.

The 'bokeler' and the 'targe' not only present an image of
the breadth of her hat but, along with the 'paire of spores
sharpe', are attributes of her masterfulness—that impulse
to have the 'maistrye' which, she will later confess,
governed her relations with her five husbands; for, in the
greatest of all the interludes between the Tales—her enormous monologue—this massive scarlet figure is set talking.

As the Poor Parson (who comes, a contrast, next to the
Wife of Bath) contrasts also with the profane ecclesiastics;
so the Plowman, his brother, contrasts with the Miller and
the Reve who are dishonest and prosperous. The Miller's
dishonesty and his ribaldry are both grounded in his total
coarseness of texture and crude, primitive vigour.

> Ther nas no dore that he nolde heve of harre,
> Or breke it, at a renning, with his heed.
> His berd as any sowe or fox was reed,
> And ther-to brood, as though it were a spade.
> Up-on the cop right of his nose he hade
> A werte, and ther-on stood a tuft of heres,
> Reed as the bristles of a sowes eres;
> His nose-thirles blake were and wyde.

The mouth seems shaped for—or by—ribaldry.

> His mouth as greet was as a greet forneys.
> He was a janglere and a goliardeys,
> And that was most of sinne and harlotryes.

The pair who come last in the diverse succession, the
Somnour and the Pardoner, are the most degraded in the
human scale; they scarcely belong to the human community. When we arrive at these predatory rogues and
vagabonds in ecclesiastical clothing, these corrupt hangers-
on of the Church, we have departed a long way from the
Prioresse (in whose presentation the rarefied delicacy of the
irony has a correspondence with her mannered refinement).

The Somnour and the Pardoner have a distorted, a broad caricature quality. Yet that caricature quality inheres in what they are in themselves rather than in the art of their presentation; excess inheres in them, the objects of contemplation, rather than in the contemplation which is as steady, as unemphatic and undistorting as always. The serene Chaucerian scrutiny certainly never rested on objects more grotesquely repellent. The grotesqueness is the greater because the pair are delighted with themselves. The Pardoner, especially, is the embodiment of impudence. But they are both, in their own different estimations, on top of the world, arch-cheats, flushed with success and the profits of their exploitations of human weakness, credulity and superstition.

The Somnour's visible bestiality confronts us in repulsive details.

> That hadde a fyr-reed cherubinnes face,
> For sawcefleem he was, with eyen narwe.
> As hoot he was, and lecherous, as a sparwe;
> With scalled browes blake, and piled berd;
> Of his visage children were aferd.

On the image of a 'cherubinnes face'—a face in itself roundly innocent and angelic—'fyr-reed', together with the explanation of why it was so, produces a grotesque, shocking effect converting the angelic image to that of some gargoyle or devil's mask.

> Of his visage children were aferd.

Once again, the Gluttony of the vernacular sermons becomes an object of detached, but none the less intense, dramatic art.

> Wel loved he garleek, oynons, and eek lekes,
> And for to drinken strong wyn, reed as blood.
> Than wolde he speke, and crye as he were wood.
> And whan that he wel dronken hadde the wyn,
> Than wolde he speke no word but Latyn.

The Latin coming from his mouth (though the explanation of why Latin does so is simple) intensifies, at the terrifying climax of his drunken madness, the effect of unnaturalness and blasphemy. The creature is aweless alike of ecclesiastical law (for the procedure of which his own familiarity has understandably bred only contempt) and of divine law.

'Purs is the erchedeknes helle,' seyde he.

This awlessness, not only of man but of God, intensifies the wantonly fantastical value of the final figure he cuts as a revelling buffoon.

> A gerland hadde he set up-on his heed,
> As greet as it were for an ale-stake;
> A bokeler hadde he maad him of a cake.

The Pardoner, an individualization of that familiar figure in mediaeval life and satiric art, is something more than another kind of scandalous ecclesiastic; he is (particularly in his role as medicine man, as self-exposed later in his Prologue to his Tale) a figure of anthropological interest. As first presented in the great Prologue, he is immediately a particular person—the companion of the Somnour—whom we vividly meet.

> Ful loude he song, 'Com hider, love, to me.'
> This somnour bar to him a stif burdoun,
> Was never trompe of half so greet a soun.
> This pardoner hadde heer as yelow as wex,
> But smothe it heng, as dooth a strike of flex;
> By ounces henge his lokkes that he hadde,
> And ther-with he his shuldres overspradde;
> But thinne it lay, by colpons oon and oon;
> But hood, for jolitee, ne wered he noon,
> For it was trussed up in his walet.
> Him thoughte, he rood al of the newe jet;
> Dischevele, save his cappe, he rood al bare.
> Swiche glaringe eyen hadde he as an hare.
> A vernicle hadde he sowed on his cappe.

> His walet lay biforn him in his lappe,
> Bret-ful of pardoun come from Rome al hoot.
> A voys he hadde as smal as hath a goot.
> No berd hadde he, ne never sholde have.

The similes of the hare and the goat, besides defining eyes and voice, connect him with these odd beasts. There is a suggestion of craziness, certainly of abnormality, in the creature which is not entirely the effect in him of drink.

But it is by the junk which he draws from his pedlar's pack, his baits to dupe the ignorant and credulous, that he is recognized as the eternal cheapjack at the fair whose impudence and success never fail to fascinate and amaze.

> For in his male he hadde a pilwe-beer,
> Which that, he seyde, was our lady veyl;
> He seyde, he hadde a gobet of the seyl
> That sëynt Peter hadde, whan that he wente
> Up-on the see, til Jesu Crist him hente.
> He hadde a croys of latoun, ful of stones,
> And in a glas he hadde pigges bones.
> But with thise relikes, whan that he fond
> A povre person dwelling up-on lond,
> Upon a day he gat him more moneye
> Than that the person gat in monthes tweye.
> And thus, with feyned flaterye and japes,
> He made the person and the peple his apes.

The impression he makes in church is then recognized for what it is, a cunning theatrical illusion sustaining his profitable role as a preacher.

> But trewely to tellen, atte laste,
> He was in chirche a noble ecclesiaste.

In church he had all the appearance of a 'noble ecclesiaste', was to all intents and purposes such in that setting. But the implications are that *only* in church was he a 'noble ecclesiaste', and that his purpose is unscrupulously to profit from posturing there as such; it is another of his successful

and profitable roles; his propelling motivation, even as a
'noble ecclesiaste', is avarice.

> He moste preche, and wel affyle his tonge,
> To winne silver . . .

Later in the *Canterbury Tales*, in the single dramatic monologue formed by his Prologue and Tale, the Pardoner becomes, scarcely less vividly than the Wife of Bath, out-
standing even among the Canterbury pilgrims, as a *dramatis persona*, a character on a stage talking and acting; the
Pardoner's role is itself that of an actor who plays many
parts.

3
THE KNIGHT'S TALE

According to degree (for the lot falls as it ought to fall)
the Knight tells the first tale. This tale may well have been
originally drafted before the Canterbury conception and
nearly contemporary with *Troilus and Criseyde* or the
earlier version of the *Prologue to the Legend of Good Women*.

> For pitee renneth sone in gentil herte.

The line, both Christian and courtly, comes both in the
Knight's Tale and the *Prologue to the Legend* and distils the
essential spirit of both poems—the spirit of 'courtesye'
impersonated by Duke Theseus in the *Knight's Tale*.

The *Knight's Tale* is an adaptation of Boccaccio's *Teseide*.
But, whereas *Troilus and Criseyde* is half as long again as
the *Il Filostrato*, the *Knight's Tale* is only about a fifth of
the length of the *Teseide*. Chaucer transforms Boccaccio's
full-scale Italian epic into an English courtly romance.
The summer of mediaeval romance was over by Chaucer's
day; yet this late romance, which is appropriately assigned
to the old-fashioned 'very parfit gentil knight', is the perfect flower of the tradition in English. (*Sir Gawayne and
the Grene Knight* is very much more than a courtly rom-

ance.) The sense that passion, death, forces of disorder un-
dermine continually the splendid chivalric order, that there
is no stability on earth, gives the *Knight's Tale* its depth.

How little separates the world of courtly romance from
the world of courtly allegory the celebrated garden scene
in the first part of the *Knight's Tale* reminds us. Here the
romance has grown out of the allegory (as the *Roman de la
Rose* itself had grown out of romance). The difference is
simply that it is not a personification who walks in the
garden on the May morning but Emily, a young English
girl.

> that fairer was to sene
> Than is the lilie upon his stalke grene,
> And fressher than the May with floures newe—
> For with the rose colour stroof hir hewe,
> I noot which was the fairer of hem two . . .
> Hir yelow heer was broyded in a tresse,
> Bihinde hir bak, a yerde long, I gesse.
> And in the gardin, at the sonne up-riste,
> She walketh up and doun, and as hir liste
> She gadereth floures, party whyte and rede,
> To make a sotil gerland for hir hede,
> And as an aungel hevenly she song.

The freshness and naturalness of the clear visualization of
the young girl springs from the comparisons with the
flowers; the conversational tone ensures an entire freedom
from conventional stiffness and accords the picture human
warmth.

> For with the rose colour stroof hir hewe,
> I noot which was the fairer of hem two.

The situation—the two young prisoners in the tower
catch sight of her as she walks in the garden unconscious
of being seen—is humanly realized; Palamon's exclamation when, looking through the bars, he first catches sight
of her—

> And there-with-al he bleynte, and cryde 'a!'

—is as dramatically (and humorously) natural and right as is Criseyde's 'Who yaf me drinke' when she sees Troilus ride by.

The *Knight's Tale* is continually on the point of moving beyond itself (as *par excellence* a courtly romance) into a further actuality that would be comedy or tragedy; yet it never completely does move beyond courtly romance, as does *Troilus and Criseyde*. It continues to be a courtly romance but with an inner tendency towards a completer reality. The source of this tendency is again recognizably in Chaucer's English itself. By comparison with *Troilus and Criseyde* comedy is scarcely present in the *Knight's Tale*; yet it is present, and present precisely when the colloquial element, concrete, commonsensical, in that English asserts itself; as (a tragic recognition also)

> We witen nat what thing we preyen here.
> We faren as he that dronke is as a mous;
> A dronke man wot wel he hath an hous,
> But he noot which the righte wey is thider
> And to a dronke man the wey is slider.
> And certes, in this world so faren we.

and when it is said of Arcite—

> In-to a studie he fil sodeynly,
> As doon thise loveres in hir queynte geres,
> Now in the croppe, now doun in the breres,
> Now up, now doun, as boket in a welle.

and of Emelye, who is perfectly unconscious that two young men (named Palamon and Arcite) are suffering torments of love and jealousy for *her*.

> She woot namore of al this hote fare,
> By God, than woot a cokkow or an hare!

The active preparations that precede the tournament, and the debates among the townsfolk as to the merits and prospects of the combatants ('somme seyde . . . somme seyde') are immediately audible to us, the buzz and hum

of a mediaeval English village or town on such an occasion. The tournament itself is as actual as a contemporary
horse-race or football match. The accent of the folk is
heard (almost comically) in the exclamation of the women-
folk at the untimely death of Arcite

> 'Why woldestow be deed,' thise wommen crye,
> 'And haddest gold y-nough, and Emelye?'

The tragic perceptions depend, like the comic, on acute-
ness of sensation characteristic of Chaucer's English.

> This Palamoun, that thoughte that thurgh his herte
> He felte a cold swerd sodeynliche glyde.

Death is realized with a corresponding sharpness as a
physical condition in which the dead person, by a sudden
vicissitude of fortune, is deprived of the warmth of love
and sociability—is cut off from his human community.

> What is this world? what asketh men to have?
> Now with his love, now in his colde grave
> Allone, with-outen any companye.

A maximum, a Shakespearean vividness and immediacy
is attained by Chaucer's English in the third part of the
Knight's Tale in the succession of visualizations (they are
the wall-paintings in the Temple of Mars) of violence,
treachery and sudden death. The images, in this Chaucerian succession, are each distinct and separate from the
other; the impact of each registers in turn its separate
shock. Yet, in doing so, each contributes to the whole, the
cumulative vision of universal violence by which the mind
is shaken and appalled—and filled with foreboding for the
young lovers.

> Ther saugh I first the derke imagining
> Of felonye, and al the compassing;
> The cruel ire, reed as any glede;
> The pykepurs, and eek the pale drede;
> The smyler with the knyf under the cloke;

> The shepne brenning with the blake smoke;
> The treson of the mordring in the bedde;
> The open werre, with woundes al bibledde;
> Contek, with blody knyf and sharp manace;
> Al ful of chirking was that sory place.
> The sleere of him-self yet saugh I there,
> His herte-blood hath bathed al his heer;
> The nayl y-driven in the shode a-night;
> The colde deeth, with mouth gaping upright . . .
>
> The carter over-riden with his carte,
> Under the wheel ful lowe he lay adoun.

It is concentrated, intense vision, as authentically *vision*—
on its smaller scale—as the *Inferno* itself. Coleridge, describing one of Dante's cantos, says 'All the images are
distinct, and even vividly distinct, but there is a total impression of infinity'; the same might as appropriately be
said of Chaucer's succession here. It would be hard to
keep in mind that what are supposedly being described
are the wall-paintings in a temple; each image in Chaucer's
English starts into immediate life. Each is no longer a
picture of an event; it is the event itself. We are told, to
begin with, that the poet saw 'the derke imagining of fel-
onye'; thereupon the abstract states, anger and fear, are
present, as persons, to our visions; and thus originates the
whole solid succession of preternaturally sharp images.
The effective presence, among these, of domestic images

> The sowe freten the child right in the cradel;
> The cook y-scalded, for al his longe ladel.

evidences once again Chaucer's freedom from the solemn
pomposity of poetic, or heroic, diction. Samuel Johnson's
comment on 'peep through the blanket of the dark' might
equally well have been made about these Chaucerian domestic images, for Chaucer's freedom in this respect is
comparable to Shakespeare's.

The speech of Saturn (later in the third part) has rhetorical repetitions appropriate to the god pronouncing doom, but still has the same freedom of diction.

> Myn is the drenching in the see so wan;
> Myn is the prison in the derke cote;
> Myn is the strangling and hanging by the throte;
> The murmure, and the cherles rebelling,
> The groyning, and the pryvee empoysoning . . .
> Myn is the ruine of the hye halles,
> The falling of the toures and of the walles
> Up-on the mynour or the carpenter.
> I slow Sampsoun in shaking the piler;
> And myne be the maladyes colde,
> The derke tresons, and the castes olde;
> My loking is the fader of pestilence.

The ruin of the high halls and falling towers and walls might occur in any mutability poem; but the addition of

> Up-on the mynour or the carpenter

lends these images their particular, their Chaucerian, force; there is also in 'drenching in the see', 'hanging by the throte', 'the cherles rebelling' and in the final personification this particular force.

4

THE MILLER'S, THE REVE'S AND THE COOK'S TALES

On the conclusion of the *Knight's Tale* the Host, 'our aller cok', calls upon the Monk, as evidently the next in degree,[1] to tell the next tale. But when the Miller, having got drunk, thereupon breaks in and insists on telling his tale next, the Host for the sake of peace acquiesces. Degree is thus dramatically broken; and by such dramatic means

[1] The Monk is 'my lord Monk', no ordinary monk, but evidently a Prior and likely to be an Abbot.

throughout the *Canterbury Tales* contrasts are achieved between the tales. The 'cherles tale' of the drunken Miller is juxtaposed with the courtly romance of the Knight. Further, the Miller tells his *fabliau* at the expense of a carpenter, which is what Osewald the Reve happens to be. This starts a quarrel between the Miller and the Reve from which dramatically a *debate* originates; for the Reve replies with his *fabliau* at the expense of a miller. The *fabliaux* of the Friar and the Somnour embody, later in the total emerging pattern, a corresponding debate.

It should be recognized at once that these tales are not mere *fabliaux*. They evidently take their rise from *fabliaux*, and even as Canterbury tales they are intended, in the farcical character of their episodes, to be representative of *fabliaux*. But they have now become art, Chaucer's maturest art, the art of a great comic master. The characterization has been realized, creatively developed, beyond that of the *fabliaux*; and the farcical climaxes and surprises that spring from and involve the characters are achieved and stage-managed with masterly dramatic imagination.

The character presentation in the *Miller's Tale* is once again the supreme art of the great Prologue, and such as is not found in the specimens of crude non-literary *fabliaux* that have accidentally survived (though the rudiments of the art are certainly recognizable in the one or two English specimens). The young wife, Alisoun, is as alive, as immediate, as vividly *there*, as the Wife of Bath. She is presented largely by means of similes, as are the personifications of the *Romaunt of the Rose*; Chaucer's method in all its development has never swerved in this respect. But Alisoun is so aboundingly alive because the similes themselves are so much more alive. Chaucer is now drawing upon and managing completely freely the creative resources of English speech; and these resources are the source of Alisoun's wonderful vitality, a peasant vitality arising from the (so largely) country imagery in which she is created, though she is a wealthy young bourgeois wife of Oxford town.

Jalous he was, and heeld hir narwe in cage,
For she was wilde and yong, and he was old . . .
Fair was this yonge wyf, and ther-with-al
As any wesele hir body gent and smal.
A ceynt she werede barred al of silk,
A barmclooth eek as whyt as morne milk
Up-on hir lendes, ful of many a gore.
Whyt was hir smok and brouded al bifore
And eek bihinde, on hir coler aboute,
Of col-blak silk, with-inne and eek withoute.
The tapes of hir whyte voluper
Were of the same suyte of hir coler;
Hir filet brood of silk, and set ful hye:
And sikerly she hadde a likerous yë.
Ful smale y-pulled were hir browes two,
And tho were bent, and blake as any sloo.
She was ful more blisful on to see
Than is the newe pere-jonette tree;
And softer than the wolle is of a wether.
And by hir girdel heeng a purs of lether
Tasseld with silk, and perled with latoun.
In al this world, to seken up and doun,
There nis no man so wys, that coude thenche
So gay a popelote, or swich a wenche.
Ful brighter was the shyning of hir hewe
Than in the tour the noble y-forged newe.
But of hir song, it was as loude and yerne
As any swalwe sittinge on a berne.
Ther-to she coude skippe and make game,
As any kide or calf folwinge his dame,
Hir mouth was swete as bragot or the meeth,
Or hord of apples leyd in hey or heeth.
Winsinge she was, as is a joly colt,
Long as a mast, and upright as a bolt.
A brooch she baar up-on hir lowe coler,
As brood as is the bos of a bocler.
Hir shoes were laced on hir legges hye;
She was a prymerole, a pigges-nye,

> For any lord to leggen in his bedde,
> Or yet for any good yeman to wedde.

The images of wild or young animals (the weasel, kid, calf, colt) convey the impression of her wild, young life. Suggestions of fruitfulness and natural growth are conveyed in the comparisons of her with the 'pere-jonette tree' and apples in hay; the 'bragot' and meed convey impressions of her freshness and sweetness to taste and smell. The images of morning milk and the swallow sitting on a barn introduce farmyard associations and suggest a girl by nature rustic, though decked out in finery as a wealthy town carpenter's wife. She has a natural wealth of her own. The images of mast and bolt suggest her native strength and uprightness of carriage—combined in her with suppleness of body—and the brooch as broad as 'the bos of a bocler' adds a suggestion of a slightly barbaric element in her aspect. But the comparison with the 'wolle of a wether' suggests, in contrast, her agreeable softness. In these images she is vividly perceptible; but something further is conveyed, the essence, the essential nature of this particular young wife. From the images springs directly the recognition that her potentialities are simply those of nature, of a natural creature, wild, young, untamed. She might have made a good yeoman's wife; she is married to the rich old carpenter of Oxford town.

Absolon, the young dandy of the same Tale, is just as vivid. The same creative resources of Chaucer's English have developed him, as a real person, far beyond the Youthe and Mirthe of the allegories.

> Crul was his heer, and as the gold it shoon,
> And strouted as a fanne large and brode;
> Ful streight and even lay his joly shode.
> His rode was reed, his eyen greye as goos;
> With Powles window corven on his shoos,
> In hoses rede he wente fetisly.
> Y-clad he was ful smal and proprely,
> Al in a kirtel of a light wachet;

Ful faire and thikke been the poyntes set,
And there-upon he hadde a gay surplys
As whyt as is the blosme up-on the rys.
A mery child he was, so god me save,
Wel coude he laten blood and clippe and shave,
And make a chartre of lond or acquitaunce.
In twenty manere coude he trippe and daunce
After the scole of Oxenforde tho,
And with his legges casten to and fro,
And pleyen songes on a smal rubible;
Ther-to he song som-tyme a loud quinible;
And as wel coude he pleye on his giterne.
In al the toun nas brewhous ne taverne
That he ne visited with his solas,
There any gaylard tappestere was . . .
This Absolon, that jolif was and gay,
Gooth with a sencer on the haliday,
Sensinge the wyves of the parish faste;
And many a lovely look on hem he caste,
And namely on this carpenteres wyf.
To loke on hir him thoughte a mery lyf,
She was so propre and swete and likerous.
I dar wel seyn, if she had been a mous,
And he a cat, he wolde hir hente anon.

The situation in the Tale springs from the characters. The
note of foppishness in the character of Absolon, in virtue
of which he deserves his final discomfiture, is accentuated
in that initial presentation to the point of burlesque
extravagance. 'Powles window corven on his shoos' produces an effect of the same order of fantastic comedy as

> Enbrouded was he, as it were a mede
> Al ful of fresshe floures, whyte and rede.

But, whereas the young Squire is a spring-like and courtly
figure, Absolon is a rather common town dandy.
    The climax of the *Miller's Tale*, when the rich old car-
penter at the cry of 'Help! water! water! help!' cuts the

rope that suspends the Noah's Ark in which he sleeps and which he has constructed in readiness for the Flood (which he has been led to believe is about to return) is explosive farce of the same order as the climaxes of the *Reve's Tale* and others of the *Canterbury Tales*.

In the comic interlude between the *Miller's Tale* and the *Reve's* we see that the Reve has ridiculously taken offence at the slight on carpenters. His rage is mingled with pity for himself because he is growing old.

> But ik am old, me list not pley for age;
> Gras-tyme is doon, my fodder is now forage,
> This whyte top wryteth myne olde yeres,
> Myn herte is al-so mowled as myne heres,
> But-if I fare as dooth an open-ers;
> That ilke fruit is ever leng the wers,
> Til it be roten in mullok or in tree.
> We olde men, I drede, so fare we;
> Til we be roten, can we nat be rype;
> We hoppen ay, whyl that the world wol pype.
> For in oure wil ther stiketh ever a nayl,
> To have an hoor heed and a grene tayl,
> As hath a leek; for thogh our might be goon,
> Our wil desireth folie ever in oon.
> For whan we may nat doon, than wol we speke;
> Yet in our asshen olde is fyr y-reke . . .
> As many a yeer as it is passed henne
> Sin that my tappe of lyf bigan to renne.
> For sikerly, whan I was bore, anon
> Deeth drogh the tappe of lyf and leet it gon;
> And ever sith hath so the tappe y-ronne,
> Til that almost al empty is the tonne.
> The streem of lyf now droppeth on the chimbe;
> The sely tonge may wel ringe and chimbe
> Of wrecchednesse that passed is ful yore;
> With olde folk, save dotage, is namor.

The theme is realized in imagery that is again predominantly agricultural; the personage Death is a character belonging to the familiar village world. ('Deeth drogh the tappe of lyf'). The traditional theme of Age is evidently deeply felt here; and it emerges again frequently and sharply throughout the *Canterbury Tales*, in Januarie, in the Wife of Bath herself feeling she is ageing. But though the feeling is evidently deeply personal (Chaucer himself is growing old) it is presented with dramatic detachment and objectivity; for it is the Reve who is here speaking, a character, and not a particularly admirable or likable character.

> Whan that our host hadde herd this sermoning ...
> 'What shul we speke alday of holy writ?
> The devel made a reve for to preche . . .'

There has been nothing specially Biblical about what the Reve has said, but it has a gravity which is intolerable to the ordinary man, and the Host protests.

The *Reve's Tale* is very nearly a match for the *Miller's* in strength and maturity. The characterization—particularly of Simkin the miller, his wife,

> She was as digne as water in a dich

and daughter—is as subtle as vivid, the climax correspondingly skilful, a quick succession of surprises in knock-about tumbling action, such as we witness later as the climax between the Wife of Bath and Clerk Jankyn and as the climax of the *Nonne Preestes Tale*; it is dramatic farce closely related to the whole meaning.

The *Miller's* and *Reve's Tales* are succeeded by the *Cook's* fragment of a Tale. In the interlude which precedes this fragment the Cook's shop becomes real to us by an unerring selection of significant detail.

> For many a pastee hastow laten blood,
> And many a Jakke of Dover hastow sold
> That hath been twyes hoot and twyes cold ...
> For in they shoppe is many a flye loos.

The place is not built up detail by detail, brick by brick,

as Balzac or Flaubert might have done it; yet we are as familiar with that shop, its character, as if we ourselves had been there. It is subtle art which can thus present its object with the minimum of means.

The Cook's fragment is only the beginning of a tale. Yet in these few lines we are presented with another vivid character, Perkin Revelour, a London apprentice. Perkin Revelour has his originals in the allegorical tradition and vernacular sermons and in direct observation of life (Chaucer has doubtless observed the London apprentices). But this particular Perkin Revelour lives in the livingness of images which again come directly from the life and speech of the English village communities.

> Gaillard he was as goldfinch in the shawe,
> Broun as a berie, a propre short felawe . . .
> He was as ful of love and paramour
> As is the hyve ful of honey swete . . .
> At every brydale wolde he singe and hoppe,
> He loved bet the tavern than the shoppe.

5

THE MAN OF LAW'S TALE

The break in the *Cook's Tale* is also the first break in the unfinished plan of the *Canterbury Tales*. In the best MSS. the *Man of Law's Tale* is what follows this first gap. But we cannot know where Chaucer would finally have placed this tale in his completed arrangement.

The *Man of Law's Tale* is introduced by some words of the Host to the company in which, though he has taken exception to the Reve's moralizing, he himself moralizes on the related theme of Time.

> Lordinges, the tyme wasteth night and day,
> And steleth from us, what prively slepinge,

And what thurgh necligence in our wakinge,
As dooth the stream, that turneth never agayn,
Descending fro the montaigne in-to playn . . .
It wol nat come agayn, with-outen drede,
Na more than wol Malkins mayden-hede,
Whan she hath lost it in hir wantownesse.

That is in Chaucer's maturest manner. But the *Man of
Law's Tale*—the tale of Constance—reads like an earlier
work which Chaucer has perhaps fitted into the Canterbury conception with little alteration. It is a tale of a similar nature to the tale of Griselda (the *Clerk's Tale*) and both
these tales (in stanzas) may have been originally composed
shortly after Chaucer's first visit to Italy, *perhaps*. Both
tales belong with a small number of tales which are distinguished among the *Canterbury Tales* by the simplifica-
tions of popular religious feeling. The pilgrimage was (as
Chaucer no doubt had in mind) a religious occasion. If
these tales—or some of them—are indeed earlier work,
they would show in yet another way that even the early
Chaucer was not simply a poet of courtly love. They remind us that his poetry as a whole cannot be detached
from mediaeval Christianity. There are lines of a singu-
larly tender and haunting loveliness in the certainly early
A.B.C. (a translation from *La Pèlerinage de la Vie Humaine*)

And bringest him out of the crooked strete . . .
And ledest us in-to the hye tour . . .

which may be matched by lines of a closely similar quality
in the tale of Constance

The whyte lamb, that hurt was with the spere . . .
The child stood, loking in the kinges face . . .

Chaucer has extracted the tale of Constance from an
Anglo-French Chronicle. But it is quite evidently originally a folk-tale that has been transfigured into the nature
of a legend of a saint. It continues to have the backbone
of a folk-tale—the persecuted princess, the malign mother-

in law, the maligned wife, the mother and child cast adrift in an open boat—but it is ensphered by the pity and wonder of mediaeval Christian legend. It has become a tale of public import also; for Constance is compelled not only to leave her parents and the folk among whom she has grown up; but to leave Christendom for heathen land where she is subjected to the spells of a 'sowdenesse, rote of iniquitie'.

Constance, like Patient Griselda, is somewhere between a personification and a person; she is Constancy, a Virtue. Her tale manifests the miraculous preservation of innocence in a world of darkness, evil, solitude and death. The strength of passionate faith in the possibility of miracles of divine intervention is accumulated behind the theme.

> Who saved Daniel in the horrible cave . . .
> Who kepte hir fro the drenching in the see?

A gentler feeling, a tenderness of pity, gives its quality to the scene of the mother and child committed to the sea.

> Hir litel child lay weping in hir arm,
> And kneling, pitously to him she seyde,
> 'Pees, litel sone, I wol do thee non harm.'
> With that hir kerchef of hir heed she breyde,
> And over his litel yën she it leyde;
> And in hir arm she lulleth it ful faste,
> And in-to heven hir yën up she caste.

This tenderness derives its quality from the mediaeval worship of Mary and her Child.

> In him triste I, and in his moder dere,
> That is to me my seyl and eek my stere.

There is the same quality of tenderness for Griselda and her child in the *Clerk's Tale*. The natural human feeling has acquired a peculiar sanctity and grace which we should hesitate to find sentimental.

In some of what are regarded as the less authoritative

MSS. the *Man of Law's Tale* is followed by a lively passage (certainly Chaucer's work) in which the Parson rebukes the Host for swearing and is himself snubbed by another pilgrim (variously called the Squire, the Somnour, and the Shipman in different MSS.) as having an unsettling effect on people's beliefs.

> 'We leve alle in the grete god,' quod he,
> 'He wolde sowen som difficultee,
> Or springen cokkel in our clene corn . . .

This last speaker then declares he will tell the next tale. On the strength of his being in one or two MSS. the Shipman, the *Shipman's Tale* (which seems originally to have been intended by Chaucer as the Wife of Bath's) has been placed next after the *Man of Law's Tale* in most modern editions. This is no good reason for altering the arrangement of the most authoritative MSS. (in which the passage does not anywhere appear and may well have been cancelled by Chaucer when he transferred the *Shipman's Tale* from the Wife of Bath to the Shipman). In these MSS. it is the *Wife of Bath's Prologue* and *Tale* which come next after the *Man of Law's Tale*, but with no concrete connection with it. *The Man of Law's Tale* must, therefore, stand by itself; we cannot know what would have been Chaucer's final arrangement.

6

THE WIFE OF BATH'S PROLOGUE AND TALE

The *Wife of Bath's Prologue* and *Tale* introduce a succession of tales (evidently intended by Chaucer to stand together). Several of these present diverse attitudes to marriage and thus constitute a *debate* on this theme.

The *Wife's Prologue* is a public exhibition of her married life, a monologue in which she re-enacts scenes and dialogues between herself and her husbands. It is a gossiping overflow of herself, assuming dramatic form. She moves without inhibitions through her conjugal past, freely self-revelatory and self-explanatory (as the Pardoner also is in his Prologue). Her 'confession', like the Pardoner's, differs from those of the confessional in that it is utterly public and impenitent. The Wife glories unashamedly in her way of life, which is opposed boldly to the clerkly prescription.

She begins by opposing 'experience' to 'auctoritee'. Her own experience, as it is reviewed and assessed throughout her monologue, has been stormily rich. The governing motives of her life, as she frankly declares, have been appetite and masterfulness, Venus and Mars. But the pattern of the comedy is by no means simply a morally one-sided sacred-profane opposition. The Wife wins considerable rational sympathy, for she is set in opposition to a meagre and barren, bookish and academic scholasticism that bolsters up age-old theologically sanctioned and authorized male prejudice and tyranny. She is thus not only an object of criticism; she is herself positively a critic, who has nature and sense substantially on her side. Her rebellious excesses—identified by the irony as such—are yet excesses of a joyous spontaneity and fertility essential to the going on and renewal of life. In her own inordinate way she represents life boldly asserted against oppressive forms of death.

The first section of her monologue is a usurpation and demonstration of scholastic method. She turns the method of the clerks against the attitude of the clerks and directs it to the aggrandisement of her carnal instincts and creature purposes. The Wife's argument is for polygamy and *against* virginity. In the manner of a clerk, but on the opposite side, she cites Biblical and historical *ensamples*—Solomon's polygamy—as licensing polygamy. She displays a clerk's forensic skill in the misapplication and misuse of quotations; and has her own profane interpretation of the Bible.

> But wel I woot expres, with-oute lye,
> God bad us for to wexe and multiplye;
> That gentil text can I wel understonde.
> Eek wel I woot he seyde, myn housbonde
> Sholde lete fader and moder, and take me;
> But of no nombre mencioun made he.

She shifts the emphasis without scruple so as to place it on her own ego.

> Sholde lete fader and moder, and take me.

In defiance of the exaltation of virginity by the clerks she enlists God himself on the side of incontinence by giving boundless application to the phrase—'God bad us for to wexe and multiplye'. In that 'us' she principally includes herself. She piously acknowledges the ideal perfection of Christ's teaching; then coolly sets it aside as being, however, not applicable to herself.

> He spak to hem that wolde live parfitly;
> And lordinges, by your leve, that am nat I.

Such is the Wife's peculiar humility; to herself, she is the great exception.

She then proceeds publicly to review her five husbands in turn.

> . . . three of hem were gode and two were badde.

The three first who were good were so because they were easily governed. They were rich, old men, whereas she was a young wife. (It is a variation of the January and May theme.) She enacts how by the sheer force of that scolding tongue which the satires attributed to the wives, she governed them and had her own way.

First we have the drama of the Wife and the rich old husbands. She presents a specimen of her aggressive complaints and accusations, demonstrating how she evoked and played on the theme of jealousy so as to wring from the old husbands licence for herself and satisfaction for her personal vanity.

> I governed hem so wel, after my lawe,
> That ech of hem ful blisful was and fawe
> To bringe me gaye thinges fro the fayre.
> They were ful glad whan I spak to hem fayre . . .
> 'Sir olde kaynard, is this thyn array?
> Why is my neighebores wyf so gay?
> She is honoured over-al ther she goth;
> I sitte at hoom, I have no thrifty cloth.
> What dostow at my neighebores hous?
> Is she so fair? artow so amorous?
> What rowne ye with our mayde? *ben'cite!*
> Sir olde lechour, lat thy japes be!
> And if I have a gossib or a freend,
> With-outen gilt, thou chydest as a feend,
> If that I walke or pleye un-to his hous!
> Thou comest hoom as dronken as a mous,
> And prechest on thy bench, with yvel preef! . . .'

The old husband's rejoinder (which the Wife also reproduces) advances the stock mediaeval notion of all desirable women, and all who desire them, going to the devil.

> Thou seyst, som folk desyre us for richesse,
> Som for our shap, and som for our fairnesse;
> And som, for she can outher singe or daunce,
> And som, for gentillesse and daliaunce;
> Som, for hir handes and hir armes smale;
> Thus goth al to the devel by thy tale.

The Wife herself is sceptical—'by thy tale'. The husband's abuse is represented as accumulating and gathering, in proverbial phrases, to a melodramatic climax, which is turned by the Wife into an anti-climax.

> Thou seyst that dropping houses, and eek smoke,
> And chyding wyves, maken men to flee
> Out of hir owene hous; a! *ben'cite!*
> What eyleth swich an old man for to chyde?

139

The force of his abusive rhetoric is blunted, for her, as coming from an old man. She advances the contrasting figure of the young apprentice (Sir Mirthe and Youthe).

> Thus seistow, olde barel ful of lyes!
> And yet of our apprentice Janekyn,
> For his crisp heer, shyninge as gold so fyn,
> And for he squiereth me bothe up and doun,
> Yet hastow caught a fals suspecioun.

The Wife's fourth husband was a 'revelour', her fifth and last a clerk. They were the bad husbands because they could not be governed; with them she was about evenly matched.

There succeeds the episode of the Wife and the Revelour. In deadly conflict with him she confesses she scarcely held her own.

> My fourthe housbonde was a revelour,
> This is to seyn, he hadde a paramour;
> And I was yong and ful of ragerye,
> Stiborn and strong, and joly as a pye.
> Wel coude I daunce to an harpe smale,
> And singe, y-wis, as any nightingale,
> Whan I had dronke a draughte of swete wyn.
> Metellius, the foule cherl, the swyn,
> That with a staf birafte his wyf hir lyf,
> For she drank wyn, thogh I hadde been his wyf,
> He sholde nat han daunted me fro drinke;
> And, after wyn, on Venus moste I thinke.

She has the vigour of the *fabliau* women, 'ful of ragerye, stiborn and strong, and joly as a pye'. As seen by herself in the enchanting glow of retrospect, she once possessed siren accomplishments—could dance to the small harp, sing with nightingale voice—when inspired by Bacchus. In terms of the Seven Deadly Sins she typifies, perhaps, 'glotonye' ('dronkenesse') and 'lecherye'; but, translated to the plane of the courtly allegory of love, she would have walked in the garden in the company of Bacchus and

Venus as 'Youthe, Beautee, Jolitee'. She passes of necessity, therefore, to the contemplation of Age; and it is at this point that we are suddenly made conscious of the profundity and rich humanity of the Wife of Bath as a complete Chaucerian character.

> But, lord Crist! whan that it remembreth me
> Up-on my yowthe, and on my jolitee,
> It tikleth me aboute myn herte rote.
> Unto this day it dooth myn herte bote
> That I have had my world as in my tyme.
> But age, allas! that al wol envenyme,
> Hath me biraft my beautee and my pith;
> Lat go, fare-wel, the devel go therwith!
> The flour is goon, there is na-more to telle,
> The bren, as I best can, now moste I selle . . .

('Flour' contrasts with 'bren', but undoubtedly has here also the force of 'flower'.) The theme of Age is deeply felt, but the Wife has her consolation; she has had her fulfilment; she has had *her* world, the sensual world, the world of the body and the earth. It has been the fruit of fierce and bitter conflict—she would have got the better even of Metellius the wife-murderer—with her male counterpart, the Revelour, for whom she has consequently a generous regard.

> By god, in erthe I was his purgatorie,
> For which I hope his soule be in glorie.

The religious imagery (she has been on many pilgrimages) renders conspicuous by its incongruity (like her unconsciously blasphemous explosive invocations of Christ and the Devil) her deep profanity.

The Wife, throughout her monologue, embodies the abuse of her sex—the sex of Eve—that was the substance of the clerks' satires against women; but she glories in its testimony to the irrepressible unruliness of 'we wemen'. The licentious gossip of the wives in secret among themselves—one of the prolific sources of mediaeval satire and comedy—issues with lively force in the Wife's portrayal of herself and her 'gossib' Alisoun. Chaucer's verse at its best, as here, is very evidently a subtle stylization of one of the primary mediaeval entertainments, talk.

> With my gossib, dwellinge in oure toun,
> God have hir soule! hir name was Alisoun.
> She knew myn herte and eek my privetee
> Bet than our parisshe-preest, so moot I thee!
> To hir biwreyed I my conseil al.
> For had myn housbonde pissed on a wal,
> Or doon a thing that sholde han cost his lyf,
> To hir, and to another worthy wyf,
> And to my nece, which that I loved weel,
> I wolde han told his conseil every-deel.
> And so I dide ful often, god it woot,
> That made his face ful often reed and hoot.

This flows into a gossiping portrayal (the whole monologue being one continuous flow of gossip) of how in Lent —the season of fasting and repentance, but also the spring season—she took the opportunity of her husband's (the Revelour's) absence to 'pleye'.

> And so bifel that ones, in a Lente,
> (So often tymes I to my gossib wente,
> For ever yet I lovede to be gay,
> And for to walke, in March, Averille, and May,
> Fro hous to hous, to here sondry talis),
> That Jankin clerk, and my gossib dame Alis,
> And I my-self, in-to the feldes wente.
> Myn housbond was at London al that Lente;
> I hadde the bettre leyser for to pleye,
> And for to see, and eek for to be seye
> Of lusty folk; what wiste I wher my grace
> Was shapen for to be, or in what place?
> Therefore I made my visitaciouns,
> To vigilies and to processiouns,
> To preching eek and to thise pilgrimages,

To pleyes of miracles and mariages,
And wered upon my gaye scarlet gytes.
Thise wormes, ne thise motthes, ne thise mytes,
Upon my peril, frete hem never a deel;
And wostow why? for they were used weel.

Public religious occasions are for her—as perhaps for the
mediaeval folk as a whole—opportunities for the profanity
of seeing and being seen. Her gay scarlet clothing that
keeps fresh because used well challenges the scriptural
admonition that on earth moth and rust corrupt.

The Wife as the widow at the funeral of her fourth
husband is a robust comic development from the popular
traditional root—the profane figure piously disguised.
The neighbours suppose she is absorbed in weeping, as
would be proper; but behind her 'coverchief' she 'weeps
but smal' for she is already provided for, and her appetite
is aroused by Jankin's pair of legs walking behind her late
husband's bier; Jankin will be her fifth.

Whan that my fourthe housbond was on bere,
I weep algate, and made sory chere,
As wyves moten, for it is usage,
And with my coverchief covered my visage;
But for that I was purveyed of a make,
I weep but smal, and that I undertake.
To chirche was my housbond born a-morwe
With neighebores, that for him maden sorwe;
And Jankin oure clerk was oon of tho.
As help me god, whan that I saugh him go
After the bere, me thoughte he hadde a paire
Of legges and of feet so clene and faire,
That al myn herte I yaf un-to his hold.
He was, I trowe, a twenty winter old,
And I was fourty, if I shal seye sooth;
But yet I hadde alwey a coltes tooth.
Gat-tothed I was, and that bicam me weel;
I hadde the prente of sëynt Venus seel.
As help me god, I was a lusty oon.

At this point she provides, if not her justification (*that* she feels no need to do), her explanation according to natural law.

> For certes, I am al Venerien
> In felinge, and myn herte is Marcien.
> Venus me yaf my lust, my likerousnesse,
> And Mars yaf me my sturdy hardinesse.
> Myn ascendent was Taur, and Mars ther-inne.
> Allas! allas! that ever love was sinne! . . .

The consciousness that natural law, according to which she lives, is in conflict with moral law as interpreted by the Church gives rise to that cry from the natural heart

> Allas! allas! that ever love was sinne!

Though explained by her as of necessity ('by vertu of my constellacioun') the Wife's rejection of 'discrecioun' and pursuit of 'inclinacioun' and 'appetyt' acts counter to the religious phraseology that she uses so freely in her speech ('god so wis be my savacioun'). Within the mediaeval ecclesiastical context she is an unconscious blasphemy; she asserts the positive value of earthly love as *she* understood and experienced it, against the prohibitive morality of the Church. (Puritanism did not begin in the Protestant centuries.)

The drama of the Wife and the Clerk makes the grand finale of the whole monologue. The tearing of the leaf out of the book—an act symbolical of the conflict between the wives and the clerks—releases the final sanguinary climax.

> By god, he smoot me ones on the list,
> For that I rente out of his book a leef,
> That of the strook myn ere wex al deef.

For the Wife's fifth and latest husband, Jankin, is a clerk and the most formidable of the five. He brings to bear against her (as representing nature and instinct) the weight and authority of centuries of accumulated erudition. The qualification has to be made that, just as the Wife has shown herself adept at the misuse of books, at misconceiving authority and misapplying Scripture, the Clerk is no more than she is a disinterested investigator of the truth. If he were, the authority of books might have been revealed as not, or not exclusively, counter to nature and instinct. But with his books—a selection of books against women bound together in one volume—the Clerk is conducting not a disinterested investigation but a war.

> For trusteth wel, it is an impossible
> That any clerk wol speke good of wyves,
> But-if it be of holy seintes lyves . . .
> By god, if wommen hadde writen stories,
> As clerkes han with-inne hir oratories,
> They wolde han writen of men more
>   wikkednesse . . .

The book he was reading aloud to the Wife on that fatal night was this compendium of *ensamples* of bad women, a Legend of Bad Women. The battle between the Wife and the Clerk, as it approaches its climax, is universalized by the reminder that it is an episode in the long war between Mercury and Venus.

> Mercurie loveth wisdom and science,
> And Venus loveth ryot and dispence.

Wisdom, however, is by no means exclusively on the side of the clerks. The Wife on her side is armed with shrewd knowledge—Chaucer's knowledge—of human nature.

> Therfore no womman of no clerk is preysed.
> The clerk, whan he is old, and may noght do
> Of Venus werkes worth his olde sho,
> Than sit he doun, and writ in his dotage
> That wommen can nat kepe hir mariage!

The Clerk masses his *ensamples* of the wicked wives of the Bible and of Graeco-Roman legend, who brought misfortune and death to their husbands, towards what turns out

to be a comic melodramatic climax, a culmination in buf-
foonery of vivid melodrama.

> That somme han slayne hir housbondes in hir bed,
> And lete hir lechour dighte hir all the night
> Whyl that the corps lay in the floor up-right.
> And somme han drive nayles in hir brayn
> Whyl that they slepte, and thus they han hem slayn.
> Some han hem yeve poysoun in hir drinke.

If we compare this with the passage of youthful Shakespeare in *Richard II* on the misfortunes of kings

> How some have been deposed; some slain in war;
> Some haunted by the ghosts they have deposed;
> Some poisoned by their wives; some sleeping killed;
> All murdered . . .

we see, besides the distinctness of its images, that the
Chaucer—though it has not the post-Marlovian sweep of
the Shakespeare which culminates in the great vision of
the mocking supremacy of Death—is contained within a
steadying criticism, a consciousness of its own ultimate
lack of seriousness which is fundamentally more serious
and more mature. Though the Shakespeare passage is from
a play and the Chaucer not, Chaucer's Clerk as presented
by the Wife is a more nearly complete dramatization.

In deliberately employing his rhetoric of piled-up *en-*
samples to madden his wife the Clerk overreaches himself,
becoming himself a fantastic-comic figure. The only
possible climax—and yet anticlimax—is a sanguinary
release; anticlimax, for the mutilation of the book and the
exchange of blows are a sudden break in the accumulated
inner tension, a release of melodramatic external clowning
as if in front of an audience in a theatre.

> And whan I saugh he wolde never fyne
> To reden on this cursed book al night,
> Al sodeynly three leves have I plight
> Out of his book, right as he radde, and eke,
> I with my fist so took him on the cheke,

That in our fyr he fil bakward adoun.
And he up-stirte as dooth a wood leoun,
And with his fist he smoot me on the heed,
That in the floor I lay as I were deed.
And when he saugh how stille that I lay,
He was agast, and wolde han fled his way,
Til atte laste out of my swogh I breyde . . .

The Clerk's immediate remorse at having almost murdered his wife precipitates the additional dramatic surprise
of his sudden total surrender. For the Clerk is after all
swayed like anyone else by his instinctive responses.

'O! hastow slayn me, false theef?' I seyde,
'And for my land thus hastow mordred me?
Er I be deed, yet wol I kisse thee.'
And neer he cam, and kneled faire adoun,
And seyde, 'dere suster Alisoun,
As help me god, I shal thee never smyte;
That I have doon, it is thy-self to wyte.
Foryeve it me, and that I thee biseke'—
And yet eft-sones I hitte him on the cheke,
And seyde, 'theef, thus muchel am I wreke;
Now wol I dye, I may no lenger speke.'
But atte laste, with muchel care and wo,
We fille acorded, by us selven two.
He yaf me al the brydel in myn hond . . .
[9] made him brenne his book anon right tho.

The Wife has won the 'maistrye' (we are reminded of the
old Holly and Ivy *debates*).

The opening passage of the *Wife of Bath's Tale* implies
her essential attitude and that of her tale. The Wife is
really on the side of the 'fayerye'. The passage implies a
consciousness of the ancient nature religion of Britain as
having been desecrated, uprooted and supplanted by the
new ecclesiastical order.

In th'olde dayes of the king Arthour,
Of which that Britons speken greet honour,

Al was this land fulfild of fayerye.
The elf-queen, with hir joly companye,
Daunced ful ofte in many a grene mede;
This was the olde opinion, as I rede.
I speke of manye hundred yeres ago;
But now can no man see none elves mo.
For now the grete charitee and prayeres
Of limitours and othere holy freres,
That serchen every lond and every streem,
As thikke as motes in the sonne-beem,
Blessinge halles, chambres, kichenes, boures,
Citees, burghes, castels, hye toures,
Thropes, bernes, shipnes, dayeryes,
This maketh that ther been no fayeryes.
For ther as wont to walken was an elf,
Ther walketh now the limitour himself
In undermeles and in morweninges,
And seyth his matins and his holy thinges
As he goth in his limitacioun.
Wommen may go saufly up and doun,
In every bush, or under every tree;
Ther is noon other incubus but he,
And he ne wol doon hem but dishonour.

It is clear that the Wife's sympathy is with the old nature
cults, with 'the elf-queen, with hir joly companye' impersonated by the 'carolling' women who, in their ritualistic
spring dances, still

Daunced ful ofte in many a grene mede.

This brilliant comic fantasy has its graver implications
(and it is, besides, the Wife's effective rejoinder to the
rudeness of the Friar at the end of her monologue).

We continue to hear the Wife's voice in the telling of
her mature tale of 'fayerye'. It is the traditional folk-tale of
the hag who is really a fair lady enchanted and who is disenchanted by the embrace of a knight courageous and
courteous enough to accept her conditions and embrace

her. But it is quite made the Wife of Bath's own; it illustrates her main theme, that a wife should be free, as she most desires, and it further amplifies and expresses her irrepressible character, interests and opinions.

7

THE FRIAR'S AND THE SOMNOUR'S TALES

Meanwhile—about the Wife of Bath—another quarrel has broken out between two members of the company, the Somnour and the Friar.

> Lo, gode men, a flye and eek a frere
> Wol falle in every dish and eek matere.

This dramatically originates another *debate* that corresponds, in the emerging pattern, to the *debate* between the Miller and the Reve. The Friar in his tale at the expense of a somnour and the Somnour in his tale at the expense of a friar mutually expose each other. These tales are again *fabliaux* with the difference that they are great comic art. A full analysis of them would again disclose the main features of Chaucer's maturest art. The dialogue between the Somnour and the Devil in the *Friar's Tale* is a masterpiece of sinister familiar tone; it is related in its tradition to the dialogues between Faustus and Mephistopheles in Marlowe's *Doctor Faustus*. The Devil will in the end carry off the Somnour; meanwhile as companions of the road they familiarly discuss theological questions the answers to which the Devil knows—and the Somnour will soon learn —from experience.

The Friar of the *Somnour's Tale* is no less masterly a comic creation than the Friar of the great Prologue. He may indeed be regarded as a dramatization by the Somnour of just such a friar as is the Friar of the Prologue, the Friar as he might talk and behave.

'*Deus hic*,' quod he, 'O Thomas, freend, good day',
Seyde this frere curteisly and softe.
'Thomas,' quod he, 'god yelde yow! ful ofte
Have I up-on this bench faren ful weel,
Here have I eten many a mery meel;'
And fro the bench he droof awey the cat,
And leyde adoun his potente and his hat,
And eek his scrippe, and sette him softe adoun.

('Sette him softe adoun' on what we know to be the most
comfortable seat because the cat had chosen it.) The Friar's
preaching and begging are, of course, related; and once
the relation between his preaching and his purposes is
recognized, his preaching (all in the most vivid vernacular)
against the sins he himself exhibits will be doubly relished
as the richest comedy.

Fy on hir pompe and on hir glotonye! . . .
Fat as a whale, and walkinge as a swan;
Al vinolent as botel in the spence.

The comedy centres in the interplay between the visiting Friar and his host and hostess, the distrustful Thomas
and his wife (on whom the Friar has his eye).

'God woot,' quod he, 'no-thing ther-of fele I;
As help me Crist, as I, in fewe yeres,
Han spended, up-on dyvers maner freres,
Ful many a pound; yet fare I never the bet.
Certeyn, my good have I almost biset.
Farwel, my gold! for it is al ago!'
The frere answerde, 'O Thomas, dostow so?
What nedeth yow diverse freres seche?
What nedeth him that hath a parfit leche
To sechen othere leches in the toun? . . .
"A! yif that covent half a quarter otes!"
"A! yif that covent four and twenty grotes!"
"A! yif that frere a peny, and lat him go!"
Nay, nay, Thomas! it may no-thing be so . .
Thomas, of me thou shalt nat been y-flatered;

Thou woldest han our labour al for noght.
The hye god, that al this world hath wroght,
Seith that the werkman worthy is his hyre.
Thomas! noght of your tresor I desyre
As for my-self, but that al our covent
To preye for yow is ay so diligent . . .'

Thomas, however, is not taken in; and the well-deserved anticlimax to the Friar's eloquence is his unexpected gross discomfiture which sends him away exhibiting the sin (Wrath) he has just preached against.

8

THE CLERK'S TALE

The *Clerk's Tale*—the tale of Patient Griselda—is clearly intended as a contrast and should not be read in isolation but in its context. As one of the tales constituting the *debate* on marriage it provides the sharpest contrast to the *Wife of Bath's Prologue* and *Tale*, on the one hand, and to the *Merchant's Tale*, on the other.

Like the *Man of Law's Tale* it gives the impression of being fairly early work, the kind of work we should be inclined to date shortly after Chaucer's first visit to Italy. It is a fairly close rendering in stanzas of Petrarch's Latin prose version. (Chaucer makes the Clerk say that he learned the tale from Petrarch in Padua; Chaucer himself might have met Petrarch, but he does not say so; he should not be identified with his character, the Clerk.) The nature of the tale itself is such that it is difficult to see how Chaucer could have altered it much without changing it into entirely another thing. Chaucer may have preferred to keep it as what it is, as he had originally translated it, a tale such as the Clerk of Oxenford might tell, admirable for the purposes of contrast.

The tale of Griselda appears to have been originally a folk tale; it retains, even as the *Clerk's Tale*, much of that character. The story of the persecution of the young girl may originally have been the story of an initiation or a process of disenchantment; her lover originally a god or spirit. Boccaccio appears to have been the first to give the tale a place in European literature as the last tale in the *Decameron*. But Petrarch translated it into 'universal' Latin, to make it permanently available to the community of educated men. Mediaeval Latin of its very nature tended to produce a moralizing effect; the tale of Griselda's sufferings, borne by her with such passivity of resignation, was moralized already (as Chaucer found it in Petrarch's Latin version, *De Obedentia ac Fide Uxoria Mythologia*) as a kind of allegory of the disciplinary trials of the soul.

It is, of course, a grotesque and quite unbelievable tale. Yet it is one of those tales which have (for reasons which we need not too closely inquire into) caught the popular imagination. It has been persistently popular, and was still being performed in puppet shows in the nineteenth century, its very grotesqueness being perhaps part of its fascination. But here we are concerned only with the tale in the form we find it in Chaucer.

Its grotesqueness to the modern mind is reduced once we recognize that Griselda in the *Clerk's Tale* is not a completely human character at all and should not be judged as such. She is, again, like Constance, somewhere between a personification and a person; she is Patient Griselda, a type of wifely obedience and patience, of one (or two) virtues to the exclusion of others. As we see her first she is a type of daughterly perfection; this merges into her typification, throughout the tale, of a conception of wifely perfection—the wife as a perfectly submissive vassal of her husband as feudal lord—to the extremity of the violence that is done to her perfection as a mother; for if, by her incredible yielding up of her children, she persists the perfect image of an obedient wife, it is at the expense of having become a very imperfect image of a mother.

Yet in the scenes in which Griselda and her child are threatened by the monstrous brutality of man in the huge,

152

male shape of the 'sergeant', whose power like Death's appears irresistible, there is a humanity and a peculiar tenderness that recall Constance and her child. In the first of these scenes in the *Clerk's Tale* explicitly Christian associations, those of the Crucifixion, are present and sanctify the human feeling (our minds are again turned to Mary and her Child).

> But, sith I thee have marked with the croys,
> Of thilke fader blessed mote thou be,
> That for us deyde up-on a croys of tree.

Chaucer's additions and expansions of the Petrarch version (and these turn out to be most of the best passages) are nearly all in the direction of greater humanization of the tale; but *too* great humanization would have spoiled this particular tale.

Griselda is indeed precariously poised between the human and the non-human. She is lent a measure of human substance as a peasant girl among a village folk and their beasts.

> And in greet reverence and charitee
> Hir olde povre fader fostred she;
> A fewe sheep spinning on feeld she kepte,
> She wolde noght been ydel til she slepte.
> And whan she hoomward cam, she wolde bringe
> Wortes or othere herbes tymes ofte,
> The whiche she shredde and seeth for hir livinge,
> And made hir bed ful harde and no-thing softe.

But even as such she is idealized (like the Plowman of the Prologue) by the Christian idea of the blessedness of poverty and of labour performed in 'reverence and charitee'. The Christian overtones arise from remote but perceptible Biblical echoes and allusions.

> And as she wolde over hir threshfold goon,
> The markis cam and gan hir for to calle;

> And she set doun hir water-pot anoon
> Bisyde the threshfold, in an oxes stalle,
> And doun up-on hir knees she gan to falle,
> And with sad contenance kneleth stille
> Til she had herd what was the lordes wille.

The 'oxes stalle', taking up the resonance from previous lines

> But hye god som tyme senden can
> His grace in-to a litel oxes stalle,

half-consciously recalls the manger in which the infant Christ was laid. The 'markis' calling the peasant girl partially seems God calling the soul; her act of obeisance to her feudal lord seems almost an act of worship. The water pot also, in such a context, dimly awakens Biblical virgin-at-the-well associations. The pomp of the marriage that follows partially suggests the soul's espousals. These echoes continue to be audible right through the poem.

> 'Naked out of my fadres hous,' quod she,
> 'I cam, and naked moot I turne agayn . . .'

Such an interpretation of the *Clerk's Tale* as a folk tale which has taken on affinities with mediaeval religious allegory and with the lives of the saints should not be pressed too far. But the peculiar tenderness of the feeling cannot wholly be explained by the grotesque facts of the story, partially humanized and made humanly pitiful as these have been by such Chaucerian touches as

> O gode god! how gentil and how kinde
> Ye semed by your speche and your visage
> The day that maked was our mariage.

The religious aura is not generated by the facts of the tale; the mediaeval religious atmosphere has worked its way in.

The common-sense attitude to the tale is fully implied by its context—its relation to the *Wife of Bath's Prologue* and *Tale* and the *Merchant's Tale*—and is also plainly ex-

pressed in the comments of the Host, the Merchant and
the Clerk himself (particularly his reference to the Wife of
Bath) at the end of his tale. A tale unusually solemn in itself—too good to be true, so to speak—thus becomes part
of the comedy.

9

THE MERCHANT'S TALE

The *Merchant's Tale* follows—and is explicitly intended
to follow—the *Clerk's Tale*. In the interlude between the
two tales the Merchant reveals that, two months ago, he
has married a wife who has already turned out to be no
Patient Griselda. The tale told by the disillusioned Merchant—the tale of Januarie and May—provides in its turn
a sharp contrast to the tale of Griselda. Unmistakably one
of Chaucer's maturest tales, it is a study, by means of
poetic-dramatic enactment, of the human capacity for self-
delusion at all stages of life (there are no fools like old
fools). Januarie's fantasies are exhibited in a clear and
sober daylight of disenchanted recognition. Having for
sixty years 'folwed ay his bodily delyt' Januarie nourishes
outrageous delusions about marriage as a blissful escape
from a life misspent.

> 'For wedlok is so esy and so clene,
> That in this world it is a paradys.'
> Thus seyde this olde knight, that was so wys.

Between that note on which the tale begins and the development that follows from it the Merchant introduces a
'digression' that purports to be in commendation of marriage. This 'digression'—and suspension of the opening
note—is in accordance with the pattern of several of the
Canterbury Tales, notably the Pardoner's in which a sermon
in denunciation of gluttony and other sins is introduced by
the Pardoner after the opening note of his tale has been
struck. But the 'digression' is not really a digression after
all; it is related to the theme of the tale and in its turn

relates the tale to the interest that is temporarily pre-occupying the company, including the teller himself, thereby enriching the drama of the *Canterbury Tales* as a whole. It serves an essential artistic purpose; it integrates the tale with its context.

The Merchant's 'digression' in commendation of marriage—if it is taken with the seriousness it seems at first sight to demand—appears to run counter to his personal disillusionment with marriage and to the whole trend and tone of the tale. But exactly how seriously is it to be taken? It is in the doubt that, once again in Chaucer, the point deliberately is. The praise of the bliss of having a wife is rendered equivocal by one or two insertions in the opposite sense.

> And yet somme clerkes seyn, it nis nat so.

Theofraste for one—though we are urged to 'deffye Theofraste and herke me'. Again, whereas 'alle yiftes of fortune . . . passen as a shadwe up-on a wal'

> A wyf wol laste, and in thyn hous endure,
> Wel lenger than thee list, paraventure.

The growing exaggeration steadily carries the eulogy of marriage away from reality towards the realms of fantasy.

> She seith not ones 'nay', when he seith 'ye'.
> 'Do this,' seith he; 'al redy, sir,' seith she.

—like Patient Griselda herself. Every man

> Up-on his bare knees oghte al his lyf
> Thanken his god that him hath sent a wyf.

We become conscious that it is altogether too good to be true. The eulogy moves along the edge between solidity and air, reality and unreality, ironically.

The opening note of the tale has only been suspended. We are reminded, on its resumption, of the false basis of Januarie's belated decision to marry; he fancies marriage as an easy absolution for the errors of a lifetime.

> Up-on my soule somwhat moste I thinke.
> I have my body folily despended;
> Blessed be god, that it shal been amended!

Once possessed with the idea of marriage, he is in ungovernable haste; having waited all his life, he cannot wait a day longer. But he is as unaware of himself and his qualifications for marriage as he is later unaware of his young wife as a person other and different from himself. A wife is thought of by him as a possession and marriage as a bargain, not a personal human relationship requiring constant adjustment. One of his reasons for preferring a young maid to an old widow is that she would (he assumes) more easily be imposed upon; it would not be so easy to impose upon the Wife of Bath.

> Womman of manye scoles half a clerk is.

But a 'young thing' would (he supposes) be as wax in his hands. Further now that he has grown old, it has suddenly come to seem to him important that he should have children, and for the purposes of procreation a young wife would be more suitable.

> Though I be hoor, I fare as dooth a tree
> That blosmeth er that fruyt y-woxen be.

The seasonal implications of the names, Januarie and May, are clearly relevant.

At this point moral allegory asserts itself with the entrance of the true and false counsellors, Placebo and Justinus, like the Good and Bad Angels in *Doctor Faustus*. They belong—as the names indicate—with the personifications of the moralities. They are spoken of as Januarie's brothers; but in their contention for their brother's soul they are experienced as projections of contrary aspects of the same mind corresponding, in the universe, to contending supernatural or moral powers. But they have also a place in the social world as two neighbours. Placebo who says

> I hold your owene conseil is the beste

157

is a type evolved from satiric observation of persons at court and has as such a further objective validity.

> I have now been a court-man al my lyf.
> And god it woot, though I unworthy be,
> I have stonden in ful greet degree
> Abouten lordes of ful heigh estaat;
> Yet hadde I never with noon of hem debaat.
> I never hem contraried, trewely;
> I woot wel that my lord can more than I.
> What that he seith, I holde it ferme and stable;
> I seye the same, or elles thing semblable.
> A ful gret fool is any conseillour,
> That serveth any lord of heigh honour,
> That dar presume, or elles thenken it,
> That his conseil sholde passe his lordes wit.

The process of Januarie's self-illusionment ('fantasye') is portrayed with maturest clarity of knowledge and execution and, in its relation to the character of Januarie, completely placed.

> Heigh fantasye and curious bisinesse
> Fro day to day gan in the soule impresse
> Of Januarie aboute his mariage.
> Many fair shap, and many a fair visage
> Ther passeth thurgh his herte, night by night,
> As who-so toke a mirour polished bright,
> And sette it in a commune market-place.

The process continues unchecked, the fantasy wantonly augmented, away from any distinct objective relation to the particular object of his eventual choice.

> For love is blind al day, and may nat see,
> And whan that he was in his bed y-broght,
> He purtreyed, in his herte and in his thoght,
> Hir fresshe beautee and hir age tendre,
> Hir myddel smal, hir armes longe and sclendre,
> Hir wyse governaunce, hir gentillesse,
> Hir wommanly beringe and hir sadnesse.

And whan that he on hir was condescended,
Him thoughte his chois mighte nat ben amended.
For whan that he him-self concluded hadde,
Him thoughte ech other mannes wit so badde,
That impossible it were to replye
Agayn his chois, this was his fantasye.

This ends in a fantastic-comic magnification of the moral
confusion in which (as we have seen) it all originated. He
fixes upon 'a mayden in the toun'.

Suffyseth him hir youthe and hir beautee.
Which mayde, he seyde, he wolde han to his wyf,
To lede in ese and holinesse his lyf.

It is radically the same moral confusion—'to lede in *ese*
and *holinesse* his lyf'—the recognition of which underlies
so much of the ironical comedy of the *Canterbury Tales*.
Even Januarie has misgivings as to whether he can enjoy
both—both the earthly paradise, which he fancies marriage to be, and the heavenly beatitude which he grossly
thinks of in terms of enjoyment. The irony is that he
should be so deluded as to fancy it possible he might.

'I have', quod he, 'herd seyd, ful yore ago,
Ther may no man han parfite blisses two,
This is to seye, in erthe and eek in hevene.
For though he kepe him fro the sinnes sevene,
And eek from every branche of thilke tree,
Yet is ther so parfit felicitee,
And so greet ese and lust in mariage,
That ever I am agast, now in myn age,
That I shal lede now so mery a lyf,
So delicat, with-outen wo and stryf,
That I shal have myn hevene in erthe here.
For sith that verray hevene is boght so dere,
With tribulacioun and greet penaunce,
How sholde I thanne, that live in swich plesaunce
As alle wedded men don with hir wyvis,
Come to the blisse ther Crist eterne on lyve is?

Confronted by this, the ecstasy of human delusion, Justinus 'which that hated his folye' can only hope that
Januarie's marital transaction may be so painfully unsuccessful as to un-delude him and deliver his soul.

> Dispeire yow noght, but have in your memorie,
> Paraunter she may be your purgatorie!

The wedding feast—'whan tendre youthe hath wedded
stouping age'—takes on both an allegorical and a mythological aspect. As a seasonal feast, realizing the seasonal
significance—spring impulses in mid-winter—of the
names Januarie and May, it is no ordinary village 'bry-
dale'. The presence of Bacchus and Venus at the feast
extends its significance beyond realism.

> Bacus the wyn hem skinketh al aboute,
> And Venus laugheth up-on every wight,
> For Januarie was bicome hir knight.

The note of mocking jollity—Januarie as Venus's knight
—in the masque-like spectacle is enhanced by the mis-
chievous mirth of Venus herself indecorously (considering
she is a goddess among mortals) performing a dance. Januarie, seated beside May on the elevation of a dais, is a
fantastically deluded character, both self-knowledge and
power of objective realization drowned in kindled erotic
reveries.

> This Januarie is ravisshed in a traunce
> At every time he loked on hir face;
> But in his herte he gan hir to manace,
> That he that night in armes wolde hir streyne
> Harder than ever Paris dide Eleyne.
> But nathelees, yet hadde he greet pitee,
> That thilke night offenden hir moste he;
> And thoughte, 'allas! o tendre creature!
> Now wolde god ye mighte wel endure
> Al my corage, it is so sharp and kene;
> I am agast ye shul it nat sustene.
> But god forbede that I dide al my might!

Now wolde god that it were woxen night,
And that the night wolde lasten evermo.
I wolde that al this people were ago.'

The juxtaposition of Youthe and Elde in one bridal bed,
the visualization of their close contact, is a grotesque
horror.

And Januarie hath faste in armes take
His fresshe May, his paradys, his make.
He lulleth hir, he kisseth hir ful ofte
With thikke bristles of his berd unsofte,
Lyk to the skin of houndfish, sharp as brere,
For he was shave al newe in his manere,
He rubbeth hir aboute hir tendre face . . .
'For in our actes we mowe do no sinne.
A man may do no sinne with his wyf . . .'
And than he taketh a sop in fyn clarree,
And upright in his bed than sitteth he,
And after that he sang ful loude and clere,
And kiste his wyf, and made wantoun chere.
He was al coltish, ful of ragerye,
And ful of jargon as a flekked pye.
The slakke skin aboute his nekke shaketh,
Whyl that he sang; so chaunteth he and craketh.
But god wot what that May thoughte in hir herte,
Whan she him saugh up sittinge in his sherte,
In his night-cappe, and with his nekke lene;
She preyseth nat his pleying worth a bene.
Than seide he thus, 'my reste wol I take;
Now day is come, I may no lenger wake.'
And doun he leyde his heed, and sleep til pryme.

May's feelings are left undescribed and may be guessed;
there is no personal human connection between husband
and wife. Even in bed with his opposite Januarie is as unaware of himself and of her and of the impression he produces, as complacently illusioned as ever; and, in his
persisting conception of marriage as licensed sin, as morally confused. The uprush of youthful impulsive joy in

Januarie himself contrasts grotesquely with his aged repulsive appearance. The realism of the visualization of
Januarie as an old man in a night-cap—Elde individualized
—has in itself the peasant vigour of the *fabliau* tales and
the Wife of Bath.

> He was al coltish, ful of ragerye,
> And ful of jargon as a flekked pye.

The impression is of some aged gnarled wreck of a tree
which surprisingly puts forth young shoots in a last spasm
of life.

The physical blindness which overtakes Januarie in the
midst of 'his lust and his prosperitee' evidently corresponds
to his moral blindness and at the same time lays him pathetically open to deception. His May is a possession whom
he guards all the more jealously in his blind helplessness.
But his garden—for Januarie also has his enclosed garden
—into which in the spring he calls his young wife in the
ecstatic phrases of the Song of Solomon, is brutally desecrated by an obscene episode.

> Lo heer he sit, the lechour, in the tree.

There are others in the garden, judicial spectators of the
episode, another husband and wife, Pluto and Proserpina, corresponding in the old mythology to Januarie and
May; and Proserpina here, in her *debate* with *her* husband, speaks uncommonly like the Wife of Bath. At the
moment of Januarie's cruel gulling his sight is restored;
but even then May successfully induces him not to believe
the evidence of his own senses.

10

THE SQUIRE'S TALE

Though the *Squire's Tale* follows the *Merchant's* in the
best MSS., there is nothing to show whether or not

Chaucer intended it to do so. It appears, in the fragmentary state in which it has been left by Chaucer, to bear no relation to the *debate* on marriage; whereas the *Franklin's Tale*, which is explicitly intended to follow the *Squire's*, includes what may have been intended to be the last words on that *debate*.

The fragmentary *Squire's Tale* consists of two episodes. The first of these, the surprising entrance in the midst of King Cambuscan's birthday feast of a knight mounted on a horse of brass, bears some resemblance to the entrance of the Green Man into Arthur's Christmas and New Year Feast in *Sir Gawayn and the Grene Knight*. But the resemblance is superficial. The foreign knight, a bringer of magic gifts from 'the king of Arabie and Inde' (originally perhaps Prester John) has nothing of the rich significance of the anthropological Green Man. The magical horse of brass is nothing more than a curious mechanical contrivance, a flying machine, round which the townsfolk congregate and speculate in an excitement of credulous curiosity ('diverse folk diversely they demed . . .'). We hear the animated buzz of their wonderment. The comedy is in the amused observation of this effect upon the townsfolk. The other gifts—a magical mirror, ring and sword—are equally the subjects of earnest popular scientific speculation. It is a very modern scene and excellent Chaucerian comedy. The note is that of the *Hous of Fame* rather than the *Arabian Nights*.

If this first episode reminds us of the *Hous of Fame*, that of Canacee and the falcon reminds us of the allegory of the *Parlement of Foules*. In this instance, however, the falcon has been betrayed by her tercelet.

Men loven of propre kinde newfangelnesse . . .

She makes her tragic love-complaint—while the blood of her self-inflicted wounds runs down the tree—to the pitying Canacee.

For pitee renneth sone in gentil herte.

163

(The line occurs in the *Knight's Tale*, the *Prologue to the Legend of Good Women* and here in the courtly *Squire's Tale*.)

II

THE FRANKLIN'S TALE

That the *Franklin's Tale* is intended to follow the *Squire's* may be judged from an interlude in which the Franklin expresses regret that *his* son is not more like the young Squire. His son will take no pains to learn 'gentillesse'. The Host interrupts ('Straw for your gentillesse'). But the Franklin returns to the theme in his Tale.

Though the *Franklin's Tale* purports to be an old Breton lay, it does not follow that it had its immediate source in such. The 'Breton lay' was, by Chaucer's time, a long-established literary *genre*. But the *Franklin's Tale* is more varied and subtle than simply a Breton Lay.

The opening theme of the tale is the very complete and harmoniously happy marriage of Dorigen and Arverigus, a deeply satisfying human relationship in which the husband is also his wife's lover and the wife her husband's lady. The Franklin's commentary on this marriage appears to express the final Chaucerian English wisdom on marriage.

> Love wol nat ben constreyned by maistrye;
> Whan maistrye comth, the god of love anon
> Beteth hise winges, and farewel! he is gon!

There comes a period of separation, an absence of Arverigus across the sea. Dorigen unable to drive away 'hir derke fantasye', her grief and anxiety at her husband's long absence, resembles as she walks by the seashore Ariadne forsaken, the distraught figure on the beach. But, more particularly, she is overcome by the sight of the black rocks that are a menace to ships.

Another tyme ther wolde she sitte and thinke,
And caste hir eyen dounward fro the brinke,
But whan she saugh the grisly rokkes blake,
For verray fere so wolde hir herte quake,
That on hir feet she mighte hir noght sustene,
Than wolde she sitte adoun upon the grene,
And pitously in-to the see biholde,
And seyn right thus, with sorweful sykes colde:
'Eterne god, that thurgh thy purveyaunce
Ledest the world by certein governaunce,
In ydel, as men seyn, ye no-thing make;
But, lord, thise grisly feendly rokkes blake,
That semen rather a foul confusioun
Of werk than any fair creacioun
Of swich a parfit wys god and a stable,
Why han ye wroght this werk unresonable?
For by this werk, south, north, ne west, ne eest,
Ther nis y-fostred man, ne brid, ne beest;
It dooth no good, to my wit, but anoyeth.
See ye nat, lord, how mankinde it destroyeth?
An hundred thousand bodies of mankinde
Han rokkes slayn, al be they nat in minde,
Which mankinde is so fair part of thy werk
That thou it madest lyk to thyn owene merk.
Than semed it ye hadde a greet chiertee
Toward mankinde; but how than may it be
That ye swiche menes make it to destroyen,
Whiche menes do no good, but ever anoyen?
I woot wel clerkes wol seyn, as hem leste,
By arguments, that al is for the beste,
Though I ne can the causes nat y-knowe.
But thilke god, that made wind to blowe,
As kepe my lord! this my conclusioun;
To clerkes lete I al disputisoun.
But wolde god that alle thise rokkes blake
Were sonken in-to helle for his sake!
Thise rokkes sleen myn herte for the fere.'

It is, to begin with, a dramatic study of an overwrought condition, the overburdened heart of the woman too long vainly expectant of her husband's return from dreaded peril. But it is the *irrationality* of the rocks (to her mind) that finally becomes what is most disturbing. They are 'a foul confusioun', 'a werk unresonable' for which the arguments of clerks afford no explanation. The anguished cry of the distracted woman is merged in that of the outraged reason. The accumulated rhythmical emphasis falls on 'helle'; the black rocks seem an emanation of evil.

The fortunate marriage is indeed imperilled by more than the sea and its black rocks. The rocks begin to symbolize that which intervenes to prevent, in the world, a positive and perfect happiness. Her friends lead Dorigen among the dancers in the May garden in a futile effort to dispel her broodings.

> For she ne saugh him on the daunce go,
> That was hir housbonde and hir love also.

Among the dancers is the infatuated squire, Aurelius—the lover of the courtly allegories and romances—to whom she makes the rash promise (of so many folk tales) to give herself if he can perform the impossible, remove the black rocks that menace her husband. Aurelius, though passionately in love with Dorigen, would more surely than the rocks break up the deep living relationship between husband and wife. Arverigus returns safely after all.

But meanwhile Aurelius has been led by his pitying brother to a clerk of Orleans who is immersed in magic. The element of magic—magical illusion is here equated with deception—re-inforces the suggestion of evil evoked by the black rocks. The magician's journey through the dead midwinter season—accompanying Aurelius back from Orleans to Brittany—is charged with menace. But even in the dead season life and reality are still at the root of the world.

> And this was, as the bokes me remembre,
> The colde frosty seson of Decembre.

Phebus wex old, and hewed lyk latoun,
That in his hote declinacioun
Shoon as the burned gold with stremes brighte;
But now in Capricorn adoun he lighte,
Wher-as he shoon ful pale, I dar wel seyn.
The bittre frostes, with the sleet and reyn,
Destroyed hath the grene in every yerd.
Janus sit by the fyr, with double berd,
And drinketh of his bugle-horn the wyn.
Biforn him stant braun of the tusked swyn,
And 'Nowel' cryeth every lusty man.

The robust figure of Janus—the old Roman seasonal god from whom the first month of the year takes its name—has here a suddenly invigorating effect. He is seen as a contemporary English yeoman by a Yule fire. He draws his strength and significance from both the immediately observed world of English agricultural life and the mythological world. His substantiality makes the decisive contrast with the magician's illusions.

Magic does indeed cause the rocks to *seem*—transiently—to disappear. But evil cannot be cast out by evil. The black rocks are perhaps preferable, accepted as a fact, to the involvements of the illusion of their absence. The rational mind—which is here, once again in Chaucer, the religious mind—insists on the distinction between appearance and reality.

For holy chirches feith in our bileve
Ne suffreth noon illusioun us to greve.

Dorigen's agony of mind when she discovers herself caught in these involvements is conveyed in sudden sharp impressions.

In al hir face nas a drope of blood . . .

And she answerde, half as she were mad . . .

She is released, and order and harmony restored, through three successive acts of 'gentillesse' springing from rich human generosity. The third of these is the act of the 'magician' himself; a clerk, he says, is as capable of a 'gentil' act as a knight or squire.

The Franklin's aspirations towards the idea of 'gentil-lesse' have—to judge from this conclusion to his tale—a substantial basis in his own genial humanity. The Janus of his tale, representative of life, would be to him a congenial figure. At the same time he recognizes an ideal of civilized living.

12

THE PHYSICIAN'S TALE
THE PARDONER'S PROLOGUE
AND TALE

There is again a break after the *Franklin's Tale*. The *Physician's Tale* and the *Pardoner's Prologue* and *Tale* follow in the best MSS.; and these, wherever they would finally have stood in relation to the other tales, are expressly intended to stand together. The *Pardoner's Prologue* and *Tale* are organically one, a dramatization of the Pardoner, and unmistakably one of Chaucer's maturest achievements.

The *Physician's Tale*—the tale of Apius and Virginia—reads not unlike one of the legends of the *Legend of Good Women*, and may well have been composed contemporaneously with these. This tale of a virgin killed by her father to preserve her virginity—a martyrdom for virginity—is left relatively undeveloped by Chaucer, though it is lent some human interest by him as a tale of a false judge and the tragedy of a father and daughter.

But the Chaucerian dramatic interest here is less in the tale itself than in the Host's reaction to it. The good-natured fellow is powerfully affected, his Englishman's sense of justice outraged.

'Harrow!' quod he, 'by nayles and by blood!
This was a fals cherl and a fals justyse! . . .'
He declares he is in need of a drink to restore his spirits,

168

or else of a merry tale; so he calls upon the Pardoner. At that the 'gentils' are fearful of hearing some 'ribaudye' and insist 'Tel us som moral thing'. The Pardoner has, as he says, to 'thinke up-on som honest thing' while he drinks. The irony is that he does indeed tell a moral tale with a vengeance.

But first, after this interlude, comes the *Pardoner's Prologue* to his *Tale*. This consists, as he drinks, of his 'confession'—a 'confession' of the same order as that of the Wife of Bath. The 'confession' should simply be accepted as a convention like those soliloquies in Elizabethan plays in which the villain comes to the front of the stage and, taking the audience entirely into his confidence, unmasks himself ('I am determined to prove a villain'). The consideration that the rogue is here apparently giving away to his fellow-pilgrims the secrets he lives by will only intervene when we refuse (incapacitated, perhaps, by modern 'naturalistic' conventions) to accept the convention—and that would be just as unreasonable as if we were to refuse to accept the other convention that he speaks in verse. Even by 'naturalistic' expectations the phenomenon is not outrageously improbable. In an excess of exhibitionism, glorying and confident in his invincible roguery, his tongue loosened by drink, the Pardoner is conceivable as sufficiently carried away to boast incautiously as well as impudently. But such considerations are hardly the relevant ones here. A conventionalized dramatic figure—such as could not be met with off a stage—is not necessarily less living or less of a reality than a purely 'naturalistic' dramatic figure. That partly depends on the vitality of the convention itself, which may concentrate instead of dissipate, eliminate all but essentials, sharply define, focus and intensify. Within the frame of the present convention— the 'confession'—a dramatization of spectacular boldness, remarkable intensity and even subtlety is presented. By its means the Pardoner exhibits himself (like the Wife of Bath) without reserve.

The themes of the Pardoner's initial characterization in the great *Prologue* are developed and illustrated dramatically in both the *Pardoner's Prologue* and his *Tale*, which together may be regarded as all the Pardoner's monologue. He combines several roles. His chief role, in which he most prides himself, is that of the fraudulent preacher who preaches against the sin which he himself typifies—Avarice. The object of his emotional and vivid sermons against Avarice is to loosen his hearers' heart-strings and purse-strings for his own profit. To this immoral end he is consciously the declamatory preacher, the spell-binder, in the guise of holiness. He presents, for admiration, the image of himself in the pulpit, incidentally revealing his contempt for the 'lewed peple' whom he deceives.

> I peyne me to han an hauteyn speche,
> And ringe it out as round as gooth a belle . . .
> I stonde lyk a clerk in my pulpet,
> And whan the lewed peple is doun y-set,
> I preche, so as ye han herd bifore,
> And telle an hundred false japes more.
> Than peyne I me to strecche forth the nekke,
> And est and west up-on the peple I bekke,
> As doth a dowve sitting on a berne.
> Myn hondes and my tonge goon so yerne,
> That it is joye to see my bisinesse.
> Of avaryce and of swich cursednesse
> Is al my preching, for to make hem free
> To yeve her pens, and namely un-to me . . .
> I rekke never, whan that they ben beried,
> Though that her soules goon a-blake-beried!

He will do no honest work (such as weave baskets). His other profitable roles are those of a pedlar of pardons and sham relics, and a medicine-man selling false remedies and formulas to induce people to feel and believe what they would like to—against the evidence of their own senses—and to multiply the crops and cure sick animals.

> For, though a man be falle in jalous rage,
> Let maken with this water his potage,
> And never shal he more his wyf mistriste,

> Though he the sooth of hir defaute wiste;
> Al had she taken preestes two or three.
> Heer is a miteyn eek, that ye may see,
> He that his hond wol putte in this miteyn,
> He shal have multiplying of his greyn . . .

Part of the power he exerts is unmistakably as a survival of the traditional medicine-man. As the eternal charlatan, show-man or quack, his roles are still being played not only in market-places and at street corners.

The *Pardoner's Tale* has the dual character of a popular sermon and a moral tale. The tale itself is such as might have been grafted on to a popular sermon on Gluttony and Avarice as an *exemplum*, to show Death as the wages of sin. It belongs (though in its origins clearly an old traditional tale) with the Pardoner's own preaching as he has been describing and enacting it in his *Prologue*. But the order by which the tale is subsidiary to the sermon is in this case reversed. Instead of the tale growing out of the sermon, the sermon here grows out of the tale; instead of incorporating the tale, the sermon is here incorporated in the tale; and the tale concludes, not only with a final condemnation of the sins of Gluttony and Avarice, but a confident attempt by the Pardoner to make the most of its terrifying effect by yet another production of the scandalous bulls and relics. The Pardoner's preaching and entertaining are entangled, perhaps confused in his own mind, share an identical lurid life, and are calculated by him to promote his private business ends.

The lurid opening of the tale startles us sensationally into attention with its images of ferocious riot, and with the tone of moral indignation which accompanies these images, a moral indignation that on examination turns out (as frequently with moral indignation) not to be so moral after all, but to be itself an accompanying emotional orgy on the part of the Pardoner.

> . . . yonge folk, that haunteden folye,
> As ryot, hasard, stewes, and tavernes,

> Wher-as, with harpes, lutes, and giternes,
> They daunce and pleye at dees both day and night,
> And ete also and drinken over hir might,
> Thurgh which they doon the devel sacrifyse
> With-in that develes temple, in cursed wyse,
> By superfluitee abhominable;
> Hir othes been so grete and so dampnable,
> That it is grisly for to here hem swere;
> Our blissed lordes body they to-tere;
> Hem thoughte Jewes rente him noght y-nough;
> And ech of hem at otheres sinne lough.
> And right anon than comen tombesteres
> Fetys and smale, and yonge fruytesteres,
> Singers with harpes, baudes, wafereres,
> Whiche been the verray develes officeres
> To kindle and blowe the fyr of lecherye,
> That is annexed un-to glotonye;
> The holy writ take I to my witnesse,
> That luxurie is in wyn and dronkenesse.

The images are presented along with a thunderous over-charge of shocked and outraged half-superstitious, half-religious feeling.

> . . . they doon the devel sacrifyse
> With-in that develes temple, in cursed wyse.

Blasphemy is visualized as an act monstrously unnatural and ghastly, the mutilation of the body of Christ.

Our imagination having been seized by these sensational means we find ourselves launched first not into a tale but into a sermon. This 'digression'—a sermon on gluttony and drunkenness, gambling and swearing—again serves an integrating and dramatic function. Not only are the themes of the sermon themes which the suspended tale will illustrate, but the sermon is a further exhibition by the Pardoner of his powers, and a further revelation of the Pardoner. He consciously dramatizes certain aspects of himself—he is a play actor by nature and

172

profitable practice—but is unconscious of other aspects of himself. He is both half-horrified and half-fascinated by the subject matter of his sermon. He unconsciously gloats over the sins he zestfully condemns. There is in his sermon (as, Eliot remarks, perhaps lurks even in some of Donne's sermons on corruption) a sly yielding to what for him is the grotesque fascination of the flesh. The dramatization here is more inclusive than the Pardoner's own conscious self-dramatization as a popular preacher, and it completely detaches and objectifies even the sermon as comic dramatic art.

After a succession of popular *ensamples* from the Bible, the Pardoner in his sermon dwells on the original instance of 'glotonye'—the eating of the forbidden fruit by Adam and his wife—and this produces a succession of indignant (or mock-indignant) apostrophes and exclamations—'O glotonye . . . O glotonye. . . .'

> Allas! the shorte throte, the tendre mouth,
> Maketh that, Est and West, and North and South,
> In erthe, in eir, in water men to-swinke
> To gete a glotoun deyntee mete and drinke!

The idea corresponds to the Jacobean idea that the fine clothes on a courtier's or lady's back may have cost an estate—evidence again that the Jacobean social conscience was inherited from the mediaeval religious attitude. The poetry here depends particularly on the contrasts arising from the conjunction of vigorous popular speech with scholastic phraseology.

> O wombe! O bely! O stinking cod,
> Fulfild of donge and of corrupcioun!
> At either ende of thee foul is the soun.
> How greet labour and cost is thee to finde!
> Thise cokes, how they stampe, and streyne, and grinde,
> And turnen substaunce in-to accident,
> To fulfille al thy likerous talent!

173

> Out of the harde bones knokke they
> The mary, for they caste noght a-wey
> That may go thurgh the golet softe and swote.

A fantastic-comic effect is produced by the virtual dissociation of the belly and gullet—as, just before, of the throat and mouth—from the rest of the body, their virtual personification and consequent magnification; and by the impression of the wasted labour and sweat of the cooks in (contrasting metaphysical phrase) 'turnen substaunce in-to accident'. The vigorous coarseness and the metaphysics come together, momentarily, in the term 'corrupcioun'. How close Chaucer can sometimes come, in some of the elements of his art, to the vernacular sermons, and *Piers Plowman* is once again shown in the Pardoner's farcical impression of Drunkenness.

> O dronke man, disfigured is thy face,
> Sour is thy breeth, foul artow to embrace,
> And thurgh thy dronke nose semeth the soun
> As though thou seydest ay 'Sampsoun, Sampsoun';
> And yet, god wot, Sampsoun drank never no wyn.
> Thou fallest, as it were a stiked swyn . . .
> That whan a man hath dronken draughtes three,
> And weneth that he be at hoom in Chepe,
> He is in Spayne, right at the toune of Lepe,
> Nat at the Rochel, ne at Burdeux toun;
> And thanne wol he seye, 'Sampsoun, Sampsoun'.

Gluttony has been visualized in the sermon as parts of the body that have taken on a kind of independent life of their own as in the fable of the rebellious members; drunkenness is impersonated realistically as a drunk man.

The tavern scene is before us again—on the resumption of the suspended tale—and has as its sombre and sinister background one of those periodic visitations of the pestilence (the Death) which made such a profound impact on mediaeval religious feeling as retribution for sin. The 'ryotoures' seated in the tavern are suddenly confronted

in the midst of their ferocious lusts by an image of
death.

> And as they satte, they herde a belle clinke
> Biforn a cors, was caried to his grave.

Death was a person to the mediaeval mind, with its deep-
rooted personifying impulse, and Death's victim is correspondingly seen as a sharp visual image.

> He was, pardee, an old felawe of youres;
> And sodeynly he was y-slayn to-night,
> For-dronke, as he sat on his bench up-right;
> Ther cam a privee theef, men clepeth Deeth,
> That in this contree al the people sleeth.

In their drunken rage the rioters therefore rush forth to
seek and to slay Death.

> And we wol sleen this false traytour Deeth;
> He shal be slayn, which that so many sleeth.

As they are about to cross a stile they do indeed meet
someone who is equally anxious for death, an old man.

> Right as they wolde han troden over a style,
> An old man and a povre with hem mette.
> This olde man ful mekely hem grette,
> And seyde thus, 'now, lordes, god yow see!'
> The proudest of thise ryotoures three
> Anserde agayn, 'what? carl, with sory grace,
> Why artow al forwrapped save thy face?
> Why livestow so longe in so greet age?'
> This olde man gan loke in his visage,
> And seyde thus, 'for I ne can nat finde
> A man, though that I walked in-to Inde,
> Neither in citee nor in no village,
> That wolde chaunge his youthe for myn age;
> And therfore moot I han myn age stille,
> As longe time as it is goddes wille.
> Ne deeth, allas! ne wol nat han my lyf;
> Thus walke I, lyk a restelees caityf,

> And on the ground, which is my modres gate,
> I knokke with my staf, bothe erly and late,
> And seye, 'leve moder, leet me in!
> Lo, how I vanish, flesh, and blood, and skin!
> Allas! whan shul my bones been at reste? . . .'

The huge power of the impression of that old man seems to proceed from the sense that he is more—or at least other —than a personal old man; that he possesses a non-human as well as a human force; that he seems 'to recede from us into some more powerful life'.[1] Though it is not said who he is, he has the original force of the allegorical Age (Elde). As Age he is connected with Death, comes as a warning of Death, knows about Death and where he is to be found.

> To finde Deeth, turne up this croked wey,
> For in that grove I lafte him . . .

('Croked wey' belongs to the traditional religious allegorical landscape.) The old man therefore knows more, is more powerful for all his apparent meekness and frailty than the proudest of the rioters who foolishly addresses him as an inferior and who may be supposed to shrink from the suggested exchange of his youth for the old man's age. The bare fact that we are impelled to wonder who or what the old man is—he is 'al forwrapped'—produces the sense that he may be more than what he seems. He has been guessed (too easily) to be Death himself in disguise. Since that idea evidently occurs it may be accepted as an element of the meaning; but there is no confirmation, though he says that he wants to but cannot die and has business to go about. He has the terrible primitive simplicity—and therefore force—of an old peasant man whose conception of death is elementary and elemental.

> And on the ground, which is my modres gate,
> I knokke with my staf, bothe erly and late,
> And seye, 'leve moder, leet me in! . . .'

[1] Yeats. *Certain Noble Plays of Japan.*

When the rioters come to the tree to which the old man directs them they find not Death, a person, but a heap of bright new florins. We are thus brought round again to the theme of Avarice. The florins are the cause of their discord and several mutually inflicted deaths. The heap of florins turns out to have been indeed Death in one of his diverse shapes. The recognition that Death is not after all a person, as we have been led to expect, and as the rioters as mediaeval folk had imagined, but that Death is more subtle, elusive and insidious—in this instance the deadly consequences of Avarice—comes as the last shock in the tale's succession of disturbing surprises.

Presuming his tale to have awakened in the company the full terrors of death and damnation, the Pardoner loses no time in producing his bulls and relics and offering them as a kind of insurance policy against accidents on the journey.

> Peraventure ther may falle oon or two
> Doun of his hors, and breke his nekke atwo.

He has the effrontery to call first upon the Host—'for he is most enveluped in sinne'—to kiss, for a small fee, his assoiling relics; but he quite loses his good humour when at last he gets the answer from the Host he has richly deserved.

> Thou woldest make me kisse thyn old breech,
> And swere it were a relik of a seint.

Yet even the Pardoner had deepened to a momentary sincerity (we cannot mistake it) when he said

> And Jesu Crist, that is our soules leche,
> So graunte yow his pardon to receyve;
> For that is best; I wol yow nat deceyve.

This final view of the queer teller of the tale sets it in a completed frame, as the peasant widow's poverty frames the tale of the brilliant Chauntecleer and makes a contrast between her sensible sobriety and his pretensions.

13

THE SHIPMAN'S TALE AND THE PRIORESSE'S TALE

After the *Pardoner's Tale* there is again a break. In the best MSS. the *Shipman's Tale* comes next and is the first of another group of tales—the *Shipman's Tale* and the *Prioresse's Tale*, Chaucer's own tales of *Sir Thopas* and *Melibeus*, the *Monk's Tale* and the *Nun's Priest's Tale*—that are again expressly intended to stand together and that compose a number of unmistakably deliberate contrasts.

The *Shipman's Tale* seems to have been originally intended to be told by a woman.

> The sely housbond, algate he mot paye;
> He moot us clothe, and he moot us arraye.

By who other than the Wife of Bath? Certainly not by the Prioress. A tale originally intended (it seems) for the Wife of Bath is therefore juxtaposed with a tale by the Prioress.

Like the *Miller's*, *Reve's*, *Friar's* and *Somnour's Tales*, the *Shipman's Tale* is again wine of an old vintage, a *fabliau* re-created by Chaucer's maturest comic art and human wisdom. The scenes—the Merchant upstairs in his counting-house, the dialogue between the Monk and the Wife, the Wife calling her husband down to dinner—are again vivid comedy.

The brief interlude between the *Shipman's Tale* and the *Prioresse's* prepares the contrast between his scandalous *fabliau* and her tale of a miracle of the Virgin. The Host has been greatly heartened to have his prejudices against monks (as suspect with wives) confirmed by the Shipman. But his demeanour changes abruptly to extreme courtesy when he turns to address the Lady Prioress and begs her for the favour of a tale. With the Monk of the *Shipman's Tale* still in mind—as well as the Monk of the company—

we cannot miss the point of the Prioress's reference in her tale.

> This abbot, which that was an holy man
> As monkes been, or elles oghten be . . .

The Prioress's tale is in honour of Mary and she begins with an invocation to Mary. There seems no reason why her tale should not have been specially composed for the Prioress as *dramatis persona*—or at least remodelled for her —no reason why Chaucer should not at a late stage have reverted to the stanzaic form and captured a note of religious exaltation specially for her. The tale is realized, within its limits, with perfectly adequate art. Though robuster than those fairly close translations and adaptations (in the same stanzaic form), the *Man of Law's Tale*, the *Clerk's Tale* and the *Second Nun's Tale* of Saint Cecilia, it belongs like these tales to what for us is a different world —not the mediaeval rational world of dogmatic intellectual belief but the world of mediaeval Christianized folk-belief; the folk, in credulous innocence and naïve wonder, confront a miracle. The ecstatic note rises above the exaggerated horror of a folk-rumour of a child murdered in an alley. The tale is one of a group of similar tales in the mediaeval popular tradition about a child murder exalted into a Christian martyrdom. The roots of the Prioress's belief are popular enough for all her social consequence.

The humanity of the *Prioresse's Tale* arises from the Chaucerian appreciation of the junior schoolboy, the 'litel clergeoun' with his 'prymer', his daily progress to and from school along the dangerous street, the 'povre widwe' waiting vainly with a mother's anxious distress for her child's return. If the tale was composed or remodelled with the Prioress in mind it may be intended to express the deeper instinctive humanity of the nun—'modres pitee in hir brest enclosed'—and to shed, perhaps, a pitiful light on her care for mice and small dogs. But the repetition in the child's mouth of the *O Alma redemptoris*—in the meaning of the Latin the child is as yet uninstructed as were the peasant folk who listened to it in the churches—sustains to the miraculous climax a quite *other* note of religious exaltation caught from the choir-singing of the church services.

> Twyës a day it passed thurgh his throte,
> To scoleward and homward whan he wente.

The child has acquired, by his absorption in the worshipped divinity, the passivity—'it passed thurgh his throte'—of an instrument. The whole-hearted acceptance of the supernatural involves in the mediaeval mind no rerejection of the role of the natural body. This perhaps accounts for what may seem to us a curiously physical, ritualistic element that is combined with the miraculousness.

> Ther he with throte y-corven lay upright,
> He '*Alma redemptoris*' gan to singe
> So loude, that al the place gan to ringe . . .

Her tale seems to show an unworldly side of the Lady Prioress and that people to her are all either black or white.

14

SIR THOPAS. MELIBEUS

The Host endeavours to restore the company, sobered and silenced by the *Prioresse's Tale*, to their natural good spirits by pouncing upon Geoffrey Chaucer. In this way a Portrait of the Artist is inserted into a corner of the *Canterbury Tales*.

> And than at erst he loked up-on me,
> And seyde thus, 'what man artow?' quod he;
> 'Thou lokest as thou woldest finde an hare,
> For ever up-on the ground I see thee stare.

> Approche neer, and loke up merily.
> Now war yow, sirs, and lat this man have place;

He in the waast is shape as wel as I;
This were a popet in an arm t'enbrace
For any womman, smal and fair of face.
He semeth elvish by his contenaunce,
For un-to no wight dooth he daliaunce.

We have had one or two portraits of the artist before—
notably in the *Hous of Fame* (by the eagle) and in the *Pro-logue* to the *Legend of Good Women*—and all the self-portraits accord with each other in disclosing, self-critically, a gentle, elusive, scholarly (but not ascetic) humane personality, humorously aware of himself as seeming to others abstracted. The self-portraits accord with the poetry; Chaucer's poetry indeed seems to be himself talking easily in a familiar relationship. The poetry reveals further that the poet's absorption is not only in books but in humanity; he is humorously aware not only of himself but of others.

Geoffrey Chaucer's own tale of *Sir Thopas* is a work of the most delicately discerning literary criticism as the purest parody may be, a parody of the highly descriptive, sing-song stanzaic lays (fourteenth-century precursors of the *Lady of Shallott*) then, in the long decadence of mediaeval romance, in vogue. The artistic miracle of *Sir Thopas* is that, within its relatively short space, it contrives to diffuse an impression of interminableness before it is stopped by the Host on behalf of the company.

It is, of course, a characteristic stroke of tact that Chaucer should cause his own tale to be interrupted. But the comedy here is more complex. *Sir Thopas*, offered as the best that Geoffrey Chaucer can do and taken at its face value (not as a parody) by the company, is not tolerated. Geoffrey Chaucer remonstrates innocently.

'Why so?' quod I, 'why wiltow lette me
More of my tale than another man,
Sin that it is the beste rym I can?'

The Host requests prose instead, either 'som mirthe' or 'som doctryne'. Geoffrey Chaucer complies with what he modestly calls a 'litel thing in prose'. The 'litel thing' is the very long moral tale of Melibeus and his wife, Dame Prudence. But it is evidently approved of by the Host as spokesman of the sensible practical folk who were bored by the flimsy, unreal romance that kept losing its way in highly coloured description.

15

THE MONK'S TALE

In the interlude (one of the vividest) between the tale of *Melibeus* and the *Monk's Tale*, the Host entertains the company with a contrast to Dame Prudence, an impression of his own savage wife rampant. He then addresses 'my lord the Monk' very familiarly as a fine specimen of a man for a woman to have children from and deplores the waste when such men become monks. In this way the *Monk's Tale*—a succession of *ensamples* of falls of great men—is introduced. Such a 'tale' is unexpected from such a character; the Monk has assumed his strict professional role. The unexpectedness is certainly intended as an element of the comedy. The Monk first defines tragedy (according to the mediaeval academic conception a fall from 'prosperitee'), then commences his solemn succession with the original falls of Lucifer and Adam. These falls (though Fortune turns the wheel) are a consequence of the sin of Pride, as is Chauntecleer's fall in the tale which succeeds the *Monk's Tale*, and is intended to succeed it, as a kind of parody.

The succession of *ensamples* which constitutes the *Monk's Tale* appears to have been modelled on Boccaccio's *De Casibus Virorum Illustrium* and may well have been composed before the *Canterbury Tales* was thought of. But the one or two 'modern instances' in the succession may have been later insertions by Chaucer. The most striking of these is a version of the Hugelino episode from the *Inferno* (Canto XXXIII). Pity is an element in the episode as it

occurs in the *Divina Comedia*, but there pity scarcely miti
gates the stony horror—though the episode has its place
in that ordered context and its relation to the love that
moves the universe. But in Chaucer's version pity as a
human response more freely and directly acts as a solvent
on the sharp edge of the original horror. The Chaucerian
pity is for the innocent and affectionate children who with
their father—conceived simply as a father and not as a
sinner—suffer the horror of death by hunger in a tower.
The children in Chaucer's version are childish—small,
helpless, hungry.

> The eldeste scarsly fyf yeer was of age.
> Allas, fortune! it was greet crueltee
> Swiche briddes for to putte in swiche a cage!

The metaphor of the birds in the cage is Chaucer's, and
so is the ascription of the blame to Fortune. The figure of
the 'gayler' (an instrument of feudal tyranny comparable
with the 'sergeant' in the *Clerk's Tale*) has also been introduced by Chaucer.

> And on a day bifil that, in that hour,
> Whan that his mete wont was to be broght,
> The gayler shette the dores of the tour.
> He herde it wel,—but he spak right noght,
> And in his herte anon ther fil a thoght,
> That they for hunger wolde doon him dyen.

On the sudden shock of that agonized recognition there
supervenes a gentler pitiableness, the common humanity
of the child hungry for its 'potage' and the father's helplessness to relieve its hunger. This dramatic dialogue is
wholly Chaucer's addition, and again expresses Chaucer's
gentleness and compassion.

> His yonge sone, that three yeer was of age,
> Un-to him seyde, 'fader, why do ye wepe?
> Whan wol the gayler bringen our potage,
> Is ther no morsel breed that ye do kepe?
> I am so hungry that I may nat slepe.

> Now wolde god that I mighte slepen ever!
> Than sholde nat hunger in my wombe crepe.

Hunger in Chaucer's English is a beast that creeps into the 'wombe'. The child's simple acceptance of death is described with an un-Elizabethan absence of fuss, a simple bareness of statement that leaves the fact salient—

> Til in his fadres barme adoun it lay,
> And seyde, 'far-wel, fader, I moot dye,'
> And kiste his fader, and deyde the same day—

and contrasts with the animal-like action of the distraught father.

> For wo his armes two he gan to byte.

But finally the repulsively horrible is transmuted into the sublimely pathetic when that action is misunderstood by the two surviving children and their love expresses itself in a self-sacrificial offer of their bodies as food that would be grotesque if it did not recall, by its phrasing, the sacraments of religion.

> His children wende that it for hunger was
> That he his armes gnow, and nat for wo,
> And seyde, 'fader, do nat so, allas!
> But rather eet the flesh upon us two;
> Our flesh thou yaf us, tak our flesh us fro.

As in other tales a mother and child, here a father and his three children in a tower, assume some of the quality, if not the meaning, of religious symbolism.

But the Monk's succession is as a whole a monotonous succession, and it is cut short by the Knight. (It is not the monotony which the kindly Knight cannot endure but to hear how so many have fallen from 'prosperitee'; he would rather hear the contrary, how a man in 'povre estat . . . clymbeth up and wexeth fortunat'.)

16

THE NUN'S PRIEST'S TALE

The Host, of course, heartily agrees with the Knight's interruption of the *Monk's Tale*; a melancholy monotony, besides being futile—there is no use in bewailing spilt milk—is unsociable, does not promote the cheerfulness of a company. He turns from the Monk to the Nun's Priest, who has not hitherto figured in the foreground, for a merry tale.

> Be blythe, though thou ryde up-on a jade.
> What though thyn hors be bothe foule and lene,
> If he wol serve thee, rekke nat a bene;
> Look that thyn herte be mery evermo.

Despite his impoverished exterior

> This swete preest, this goodly man, sir John

does indeed tell a blithe, a witty and wise tale, the tale of Chauntecleer and Pertelote; surely Chaucer's masterpiece among the *Canterbury Tales*.

For only a refusal to allow that a tale purporting to be about a cock and a hen could be more than light entertainment with an improving 'moral' added (though its 'skill' as a little masterpiece of comic 'art' might be admired) could have hindered recognition of the moral fable of Chauntecleer and Pertelote as a great and wise poem about human nature, a humane masterpiece. The inclusiveness of the harmony of the poem, the diversity of spheres of human experience and knowledge involved and composed in the harmony, constitutes it perhaps the wisest single poem of all the *Canterbury Tales* and therefore perhaps the supreme expression—and the most urbane expression—of the mediaeval English organic community.

> When England, old already, was called merry.[1]

[1] Edward Thomas: *The Manor Farm.*

Against the sober realistic background of a peasant
widow's poverty, and in contrast to her prudent wisdom,
is set the mock-heroic brilliance of the dazzling cock.

> His vois was merier than the mery orgon
> On messe-dayes that in the chirche gon;
> Wel sikerer was his crowing in his logge,
> Than is a clokke, or an abbey orlogge . . .
> His comb was redder than the fyn coral,
> And batailed, as it were a castel-wal.
> His bile was blak, and as the jeet it shoon;
> Lyk asur were his legges, and his toon;
> His nayles whytter than the lilie flour,
> And lyk the burned gold was his colour.

The splendid comparisons (and colours) lavished inordin-
ately upon a cock produce a burlesque in which the gorge-
ous creature is seen as a proud—perhaps vainglorious—
prince of a romance or 'tragedy'; particularly, the glorification of his crowing draws attention at once to that gift
of which he is especially vain and which is to be the agency
of his fall. Thus is introduced what is to prove the tale's
central theme of pride—the pride that goes before a fall.
The position of the *Nun's Priest's Tale* immediately after
the Monk's solemn succession of tragic instances—

> Of him that stood in greet prosperitee
> And is y-fallen out of heigh degree

—indicates that it is intended (among other things) to
parody these; but the comedy of the *Nun's Priest's Tale* is
more serious than the solemnity of the Monk's 'tragedies'.
    This impression of a court in a farmyard, a castle in a
hen-house, Chauntecleer a knight, Pertelote his lady,
shifts into a domestic scene between the cock and hen
couple—a most natural parody of a human husband and
wife. The scene engages the fullest human sympathy for
Chauntecleer and Pertelote. When Pertelote says to
Chauntecleer (badly shaken by a dream he has had in the

night of that beast which we recognize from his description is a fox)

> Now han ye lost myn herte and al my love;
> I can nat love a coward, by my feith . . .
> Have ye no mannes herte, and han a berd?

they are the very words of a wife. The human conjugal relation is rendered the more piquant by the attribution of a man's heart and beard to—when we remember—a cock. But Chauntecleer is more than an aspect of humanity, the cock-like strutting male aspect; Pertelote more than the hen-like female aspect; they are individuals, they are distinct, rounded characters.

The cock and hen *debate* on dreams (like the *debate* on the same theme between Troilus and Pandarus) brings out the contrast between them; it is the old *debate* in a new comic setting. Pertelote is the practical wife. She ascribes a purely physiological cause and significance to dreams and advises a laxative. She has a wealth of knowledge of medicine, of remedies and herbs, at her finger-tips. The diet of worms which she prescribes to be taken before the herbs is (we are told by the scholars) prescribed in Dioscorides as a remedy for the tertian fever which she fears her husband may have contracted; it is, besides, quite the appropriate diet for a cock. The cock thereupon displays himself as a great clerk. He brings to bear his more ponderous erudition, 'ensamples' out of 'olde bokes' of dreams that came true. These vivid and terrifying anecdotes of violent death serve the purpose in the tale of intensifying the suspense, the sense of something dreadful about to happen, an impending catastrophe to Chauntecleer. In the end he rejects the laxatives not after all on any very rational grounds but simply because they are disagreeable.

> I hem defye, I love hem never a del.

He turns instead to earthly pleasures to distract him, and first to female beauty—which to a cock is that of a hen.

> For whan I see the beautee of your face,
> Ye ben so scarlet-reed about your yën,
> It maketh al my drede for to dyen.

But even while his wife's beauty provides him with solace
the conceited fellow continues privately to despise her
because she does not know Latin, and takes a mean advantage of her ignorance to quote at her expense a Latin allusion to Eve and the Fall; the centuries-old male grimace
heightens the bookish cock's own absurdity. The scene
exposes the vanity of pedantry, and thus further develops
the principal theme of pride.

The coming of day totally dissolves, for Chauntecleer,
the disagreeableness of the dream.

> . . . he fley doun fro the beem,
> For it was day, and eek his hennes alle.

In the bright daylight as he struts before his wives and
paramours he is no longer afraid. We are made aware again
of the 'royal' aspect of Chauntecleer; his looks are the
looks of a lion.

> He loketh as it were a grim leoun;
> And on his toos he rometh up and doun,
> Him deyned not to sette his foot to grounde.
> He chukketh, whan he hath a corn y-founde,
> And to him rennen thanne his wyves alle.
> Thus royal, as a prince is in his halle . . .

When at length the fatal day arrives Chauntecleer is
once again seen as a prince about to fall through pride.

> . . . Chauntecleer, in al his pryde,
> His seven wyves walking by his syde—

walking through an earthly—and (as it unhappily proves)
a fool's—paradise.

> Madame Pertelote, my worldes blis,
> Herkneth thise blisful briddes how they singe,
> And see the fresshe floures how they springe;
> Ful is myn herte of revel and solas.

The Nun's Priest—for the tale is dramatically his—here
interposes the warning reminder

> But sodeinly him fil a sorweful cas;
> For ever the latter ende of joye is wo.
> God woot that worldly joye is sone ago.

In Chauntecleer's paradise the serpent is a fox. The fox
lurking among the plants is a type of the betrayer; and is
identified (in a passage in which the *apostrophe, exclamatio*
and *exempla* of the mediaeval rhetoric are parodied) with
the great historical traitors.

> O false mordrer, lurking in thy den!
> O newe Scariot, newe Genilon!
> False dissimilour, O Greek Sinon,
> That broghtest Troye al outrely to sorwe!

In the ensuing scene with the fox as the tempter, the serpent in paradise, the poem develops as a tragi-comic
allegory of the Fall, the major human catastrophe. An
allusion to Adam and Eve brings in the relevant associations.

> Wommannes counseil broghte us first to wo,
> And made Adam fro paradys to go,
> Ther-as he was ful mery, and wel at ese.

(From the blame of women the teller of the tale, being a
nun's priest, is careful to dissociate himself.) The earthly
paradise then vividly recurs with the fox in the role of the
serpent among the flowers.

> Agayn the sonne; and Chauntecleer so free
> Song merier than the mermayde in the see . . .
> And so bifel that, as he caste his yë,
> Among the wortes, on a boterflye,
> He was war of this fox that lay ful lowe.

The temptation is conducted with the smooth, accomplished flattery of the false courtier.

> He wolde han fled, but that the fox anon
> Seyde, 'Gentil sire, allas! wher wol ye gon?

Be ye affrayed of me that am your freend?
Now certes, I were worse than a feend,
If I to yow wolde harm or vileinye.
I am nat come your counseil for t'espye;
But trewely, the cause of my cominge
Was only for to herkne how that ye singe.
For trewely ye have as mery a stevene
As eny aungel hath, that is in hevene;
Therwith ye han in musik more felinge
Than hadde Boëce, or any that can singe.
My lord your fader (god his soule blesse!)
And eek your moder, of hir gentilesse,
Han in myn hous y-been, to my gret ese;
And certes, sire, ful fayn wolde I yow plese.
But for men speke of singing, I wol saye,
So mote I brouke wel myn eyen tweye,
Save yow, I herde never man so singe,
As dide your fader in the morweninge;
Certes, it was of herte, al that he song.
And for to make his voys the more strong,
He wolde so peyne him, that with bothe his yën
He moste winke, so loude he wolde cryen,
And stonden on his tiptoon ther-with-al,
And strecche forth his nekke long and smal . . .
Now singeth, sire, for seinte Charitee,
Let see, conne ye your fader countrefete?

Chauntecleer, unconscious of the double meanings in the
fox's (the fiend's) speech, 'is ravished with his flaterye'.
(The Nun's Priest here interposes an admonition against
flatterers.

    Allas! ye lordes, many a fals flatour
    Is in your courtes, and many a losengeour.)[1]

In this instance it is Adam (not Eve) who falls, through his
personal vanity; vanity of crowing is his downfall.

 [1] We may compare the court of the God of Love in the *Prolouge* to the
Legend of Good Women

    For in your court is many a losengeour . , .

> This Chauntecleer stood hye up-on his toos,
> Strecching his nekke, and heeld his eyen cloos,
> And gan to crowe loude for the nones.

The fantastic braggadocio creature is caught by the out-stretched neck.

The reflections on the event, though necessarily mock-serious when that event is a tragic disaster to a cock, are just as applicable to the affairs of a cock as to human affairs. The age-old *debate* of the Schoolmen concerning free choice and necessity (which the lurking proximity of the fox had earlier in the tale called to mind) now finds its response in the recognition of this fresh instance of the inexorable chain of cause and effect which involves both cocks and men.

> O destinee, that mayst nat been eschewed!
> Allas, that Chauntecleer fleigh fro the bemes!
> Allas, his wyf ne roghte nat of dremes!
> And on a Friday fil al this meschaunce.
> O Venus, that art goddesse of plesaunce,
> Sin that thy servant was this Chauntecleer,
> And in thy service dide al his poweer,
> More for delyt, than world to multiplye.

The drop from high philosophic meditation on destiny to the shocked, but hardly philosophic, consideration that the fatal day was a Friday (Venus's day) and the reference to Chauntecleer as Venus's servant 'more for delyt, than world to multiplye', are rippling comic surface variation over the poem's graver depth. The apostrophes to 'des-tinee' and Venus are anticlimaxed by an apostrophe to Gaufred (a celebrated mediaeval teacher of rhetoric) whose rhetorical aid is invoked to 'chyde the Friday'.[1]

From this parody of the apostrophes and exclamations

---

[1] 'Every educated man remembered Master Gaufred,' says Professor Manly, 'and some perhaps knew by heart his famous lamentation (on the death of Richard Cœur de Lion who received his fatal wound on a Friday) for the *Nova Poetria* was one of the principal textbooks on rhetoric . . . studied in the schools.'

of the academic rhetoric which Chaucer was himself sufficiently well grounded in to be able to treat lightly (and deliberately to prefer, in his poetry, 'pleyn' English which all 'may understonde') the poetry rises to a superb mock-heroic climax—a succession of *ensamples* in which the cries of the bereaved hens sound like the lamentations of famous women on the grand tragic occasions of history.

> Certes, swich cry ne lamentacioun
> Was never of ladies maad, whan Ilioun
> Was wonne, and Pirrus with his streite swerd,
> Whan he hadde hent king Priam by the berd,
> And slayn him (as saith us *Eneydos*),
> As maden alle the hennes in the clos,
> Whan they had seyn of Chauntecleer the sighte.
> But sovereynly dame Pertelote shrighte,
> Ful louder than dide Hasdrubales wyf,
> Whan that hir housbond hadde lost his lyf,
> And that the Romayns hadde brend Cartage;
> She was so ful of torment and of rage,
> That wilfully into the fyr she sterte,
> And brende hir-selven with a stedfast herte.
> O woful hennes, right so cryden ye,
> As, whan that Nero brende the citee
> Of Rome, cryden senatoures wyves,
> For that hir housbondes losten alle hir lyves.

This in its turn leads up to the grand climax in external action—as are the climaxes of other tales and of the Wife of Bath's monologue—moral disorder, the universal chaos of the Fall as burlesque, a commotion in an English farmyard.

> Ran Colle our dogge, and Talbot, and Gerland,
> And Malkin, with a distaf in hir hand;
> Ran cow and calf, and eek the verray hogges
> So were they fered for berking of the dogges
> And shouting of the men and wimmen eke,
> They ronne so, hem thoughte hir herte breke.
> They yelleden as feendes doon in helle;

The dokes cryden as men wolde hem quelle;
The gees for fere flowen over the trees;
Out of the hyve cam the swarm of bees;
So hidous was the noyse, a! *benedicite!* . . .
Of bras thay broghten bemes, and of box,
Of horn, of boon, in whiche they blewe and
     pouped,
And therwithal thay shryked and they houped;
It semed as that heven sholde falle.

This comic chaos is given a contemporary reference by an allusion to Jack Straw and to the disorder with which Chaucer's social world had been threatened. The hullabaloo is, by itself, to no purpose. The last-moment reversal of fortune by which the lost cock is saved springs from Chauntecleer's own wit—now that he is wiser—in successfully appealing to the confident vanity of Reynard in *his* turn. When the Nun's Priest remarked 'My tale is of a cok' that was his modesty; this fable of the fall of a cock, this tragi-comic allegory of the Fall of Man, illustrates some central truths about human nature with subtle irony and humane wisdom.

17

THE SECOND NUN'S TALE

There is again a break after the *Nun's Priest's Tale*. A legend of St. Cecilia from the *Legenda Aurea* comes next in the best MSS. (as the *Second Nun's Tale*) and is evidently intended to precede the *Canon's Yeoman's Prologue* and *Tale*. It is a tale of the same order as the tales of Constance and Patient Griselda and the *Prioresse's Tale*; it is quite likely an early stanzaic work that has been incorporated with little modification into the *Canterbury Tales*, and aids the other religious and near-religious tales to associate the *Canterbury Tales* with the religious occasion the Pilgrimage was.

An invocation to the Virgin (a paraphrase of St. Bernard's address to Mary at the beginning of the last canto of the *Paradiso*) precedes the Tale.

> Thou mayde and mooder, doghter of thy sone.

The tale itself is more of a bookish product, less of a folk tale, than the *Prioresse's Tale*. We encounter again an other-earthly note—'ther is better lyf in other place'—or, more exactly, a combined earthly other-earthly, sensory supersensory note. An angel—

> I have an aungel which that loveth me

—has brought Cecile and Valerian roses and lilies from Paradise that evidently signify particular virtues. Valerian's brother, Tiburce, smells their odour.

> And seyde, 'I wondre, this tyme of the yeer,
> Whennes that sote savour cometh so
> Of rose and lilies that I smelle heer . . .
> The sote smel that in myn herte I finde
> Hath chaunged me al in another kinde.'

There follows the beautiful and profound metaphysical recognition

> Tiburce answerde, 'seistow this to me
> In soothnesse, or in dreem I herkne this?'
> 'In dremes,' quod Valerian, 'han we be
> Unto this tyme, brother myn, y-wis.
> But now at erst in trouthe our dwelling is.'

The climax of the tale is the triumphant martydrom of St. Cecilia.

18

THE CANON'S YEOMAN'S
PROLOGUE AND TALE

The *Canon's Yeoman's Prologue* presents an unexpected and lively dramatic episode. The Canon and his Yeoman, who ride up in hot pursuit of the company in the hope of joining in, are a sudden intrusion, an interruption of the steady progression of the pilgrimage. The episode has been regarded as an interesting, an exciting after-thought. But that the Canon and his Yeoman do not occur in the *Prologue to the Canterbury Tales* does not prove that they were an after-thought; they could have no place in the great *Prologue* if their role was to surprise the company with their appearance at a later stage. Whether or not pre-visioned from the beginning, the episode is a striking dramatic development in the *Canterbury Tales*.

The Canon and his Yeoman are both seen with Chaucerian distinctness. Yet the Canon at least, despite his visual distinctness, weighs upon us as a mystery. We wonder who or what he might be.

> Is he a clerk or noon? Tel what he is?

The *Canon's Yeoman's Tale* is the exposure of his mystery; it is another study of the baneful strength of a delusion. The Yeoman in the Prologue to his Tale begins by suggesting that his master is a quite exceptional, a super-naturally potent personality. But it soon becomes apparent that the Yeoman is himself ceasing to be sure of this. His belief in his master has evidently reached breaking-point and it rapidly breaks under the shrewd, commonsensical queries of the Host.

> 'Why artow so discoloured of thy face?' . . .
> 'I am so used in the fyr to blowe.

His master is an alchemist. A public exposure of his master's, and his own, delusions ensues.

The *Canon's Yeoman's Prologue* and *Tale* are, together, the Yeoman's 'confession'—a 'confession' of the same order as the Wife of Bath's and the Pardoner's. The morbidly mistrustful Canon, who rides off overcome with guilty shame as soon as he overhears the preliminaries of his disloyal servant's 'confession', is yet elevated by the uncalculating fanaticism of his delusion beyond the sinister

sordid environment (described by the Yeoman) his delusion has reduced him to.

> Wher dwellen ye, if it to telle be?'
> 'In the suburbes of a toun,' quod he,
> 'Lurkinge in hernes and in lanes blinde,
> Wher-as thise robbours and thise theves by kinde
> Holden hir privee fereful residence,
> As they that dar nat shewen hir presence;
> So faren we, if I shal seye the sothe.'

The undeceived Yeoman, in contrast to his deluded master, is a gross character. Yet even the Yeoman, the failure
of whose avaricious calculations has caused him at length
to abandon his deluded master, testifies to the persistent
strength of the delusion.

> Yet is it fals, but ay we han good hope
> It for to doon, and after it we grope.
> But that science is so fer us biforn,
> We mowen nat, al-though we hadde it sworn,
> It overtake, it slit awey so faste;
> It wol us maken beggers atte laste.'

The serpentine deceptiveness of the 'science'—it is felt as
a creature—its uncanny elusiveness such words as 'slyd-
ing' and 'elvish' suggest.

> That slyding science hath me maad so bare . . .
> Our elvish craft, we semen wonder wyse,
> Our termes been so clergial and so queynte.

Semen but are not.

The *Canon's Yeoman's Tale* is in two parts; and the first
of these is substantially the Yeoman's 'confession'. The
principal effects here answer to an account equivalent to
L. C. Knights's of some of the characteristic effects of Ben
Jonson's *Alchemist*—evidence again of the continuity of
the English tradition from Chaucer to Shakespeare and
Ben Jonson. The successive pilings-up of chemical and
other technical terminology' is like the inflating of a

self-important exaggerated balloon to the point of over-inflation at which it bursts.

> The pot to-breketh, and farewel! al is go!

The first accumulation bursts in a recognition of the labour and substance wasted.

> For lost is al our labour and travayle,
> And al the cost, a twenty devel weye.

But the misguided effort, represented by a renewed piling-up of scientific terminology, begins afresh. It exposes itself as a scientific specialist drive, uncontrolled by humane intelligence as to ends, such as we have grown familiar with as a phenomenon of our own day; it certainly involves much relentless, but humanly fruitless, learning and hard work.

> Though he sitte at his book bothe day and night,
> In lernyng of this elvish nyce lore,
> All is in veyn, and parde, mochel more!

Though related to the illusory prospect of ultimate worldly riches, the obsession grows into an unworldly frenzy.

> . . . for nadde they but a shete
> Which that they mighte wrappe hem inne a-night,
> And a bak to walken inne by day-light,
> They wolde hem selle and spenden on this craft;
> They can nat stinte til no-thing be laft.

As reproduced in the derisive folk imagination (here the Yeoman's) the alchemists, with the smell of chemicals perpetually about them, are farcically distorted into caricatures; like devils they are identifiable by the smell of brimstone that surrounds them.

> And evermore, wher that ever they goon,
> Men may hem knowe by smel of brimstoon;
> For al the world, they stinken as a goot.

The explosion that shatters the experiment is more than an

197

explosion of chemicals; it is an explosion of illusory hopes and pretensions and of the evil passions lurking beneath and around these.

> The pot to-breketh, and farewel! al is go!
> Thise metals been of so greet violence,
> They percen so, and thurgh the wal they goon,
> And somme of hem sinken in-to the ground,
> (Thus han we lost by tymes many a pound)
> And somme are scatered al the floor aboute,
> Somme lepe in-to the roof; with-outen doute,
> Though that the feend noght in our sighte him
>   shewe,
> I trowe he with us be, that ilke shrewe! . . .
> Som seyde, it was long on the fyr-making,
> Som seyde, nay! it was on the blowing;
> (Than was I fered, for that was myn office);
> 'Straw!' quod the thridde, 'ye been lewed and
>   nyce,
> It was nat tempred as it oghte be.'
> 'Nay!' quod the ferthe, 'stint, and herkne
>   me; . . .'
> I can nat telle wher-on it was long,
> But wel I wot greet stryf is us among . . .

So the moral emerges

> And in our madnesse evermore we rave.
> And whan we been togidres everichoon,
> Every man semeth a Salomon.
> But al thing which that shyneth as the gold
> Nis nat gold, as that I have herd it told;
> Ne every appel that is fair at yë
> Ne is nat good, what-so men clappe or crye.
> Right so, lo! fareth it amonges us;
> He that semeth the wysest, by Jesus!
> Is most fool, whan it cometh to the preef.

As with the harlequinade at the end of the *Nun's Priest's Tale* the externalized confusion projects an original moral confusion and spectacularly exposes it.

The second part of the *Canon's Yeoman's Tale* consists of an anecdote about *another* Canon, a foil to the Yeoman's Canon; this other kind of alchemist (though he is associated by the Yeoman with the great betrayers of mankind) is a mere cunning imposter who gulls a priest.

19

THE MANCIPLE'S PROLOGUE
AND TALE

The *Manciple's Prologue* and *Tale* are the last verse pieces in the MSS., but remain without any connections with any other tale or prologue. The episode of the drunken Cook who falls in the mire (the *Manciple's Prologue*) is one of the vividest of the comic dramatic interludes. The realism is again close to that of the popular sermons on the Seven Deadly Sins; but the tone, as the episode concludes —the Cook being given another drink to humour him— is very different.

> . . . I have heer, in a gourde,
> A draught of wyn, ye, of a rype grape.

The Host blesses Bacchus

> O thou Bachus, y-blessed be thy name,
> That so canst turnen ernest in-to game!

In the *Manciple's Tale*, a fable of a tell-tale crow (based on Ovid's version in *Metamorphoses II*) Chaucer exhibits a formal, almost mannered, wit; it is occasionally as if he were nearly anticipating the kind of sophistication his couplet verse was to undergo at the end of the seventeenth century.

> Lat take a cat, and fostre him wel with milk,
> And tendre flesh, and make his couche of silk,
> And lat him seen a mous go by the wal;

199

Anon he weyveth milk, and flesh, and al,
And every deyntee that is in that hous,
Swich appetyt hath he to ete a mous.

We cannot say that the wit of La Fontaine is more sophisticated.

20

THE PARSON'S TALE

The *Parson's Tale*—simply a prose sermon on penitence and the Seven Deadly Sins (which have underlain so much of the comedy)—comes last of all the tales in the MSS., and it may well be that it was intended to remain as the conclusion of the whole *Canterbury Tales*.

To knitte up al this feeste, and make an ende.
And Jesu, for his grace, wit me sende
To shewe yow the wey, in this viage,
Of thilke parfit glorious pilgrimage
That highte Jerusalem celestial.

It is not, however, the final thing in the MSS. Last of all has been added Geoffrey Chaucer's 'retraccioun' of his 'translaciouns and endytinges of worldly vanitees' naming all his important, all his great poems. It need not perplex us. It is simply, no doubt, part of Geoffrey Chaucer's formal renunciation of the world as he prepared himself, or was prepared, under the guidance of Holy Church, for his departure from the world. His poetry remains. The whole movement and animation of the *Canterbury Tales* goes on.

CONCLUSION

I

The term 'poetry' has had in recent times a limiting suggestion. Chaucer is indeed properly to be called a poet; but he bears a closer relation to the great English novelists than to Spenser.

To see the poetry of Chaucer only in relation to that part of English literature which is in verse—and only the non-dramatic verse at that—is, however, less injurious perhaps than the academic tendency to separate it from the whole of what is often called 'modern' English literature (meaning English literature since the sixteenth century). It is a tendency which is limiting both to our reading of Chaucer and to our reading of modern English literature. Modern English literature is implied in the poetry of Chaucer and (we may add) of Chaucer's English contemporaries.

The scholarship which is preoccupied with exposing the derivativeness of Chaucer's poetry tends also to obscure the remarkable newness of what Chaucer has done. How new Chaucer's poetry is it is difficult for us to apprehend because so many of the remarkable developments in English literature since—and each original author has been a new development—have been developments from what Chaucer did for the first time. The *Canterbury Tales* and *Troilus and Criseyde* are, if one thinks back to what there was before them which *they* are developments from, surprisingly new works of art.

With *Troilus and Criseyde* and the *Canterbury Tales* Chaucer inaugurates the English novel; and, moreover, the Great Tradition of it. In these two great dramatic-poetic novels we see the English novel actually in being, with the characteristics of our eighteenth- and nineteenth-century masterpieces. Chaucer's preoccupations here are those of the great novelists. He explores the theme of the individual's relation to the society in which he lives; launches the comedy of the clash of character and the conflict of interests and moeurs; and shows the comic and ironic effects obtainable from the class distinctions felt by the newly emerged bourgeoisie associated with the growth of town life and of the trades and commerce (the Wife of Bath is the new bourgeois wife asserting her independence). He observes, as do Jane Austen and George Eliot, the changes in manners and outlook between the older generation and the new—between the Knight and his son, and the Franklin and his—and, like these novelists and Richardson before them, he explores feminine psychology. He develops to the highest artistic level what is only visible in an elementary form elsewhere in his contemporaries (in the play-cycles and Langland) the kind of characterization which distinguishes the English novel from Bunyan to Henry James—characters which, while exquisitely realistic in detail, are morally and socially typical.

In the final relative placing of these two masterpieces of Chaucer's art the greater variety and fertility of the *Canterbury Tales* must be taken into account. We must grant the value of the completed unity of *Troilus and Criseyde*—its singleness as a work of art—and the clarity of its final judgment on human life and love as not self-contained and as in themselves unstable. Yet the unity of *Troilus and Criseyde* is not more complete—and not more inclusive, not more complex—than that of several of the individual tales, though these are much more brief.

To argue that because the evidence indicates that *Troilus and Criseyde* was more read in the fifteenth century than the *Canterbury Tales* we should hesitate to reverse the judgment of those who were more nearly Chaucer's contemporaries than we, is surely nothing to the point. We cannot be absolved from our own responsibility—with the whole of English literature now *there* for comparison—to judge which of the two poems is from our point of view the better. We stand—or fall—by our judgments. Many of our judgments other than those related to Chaucer are no doubt divergent from those of the fifteenth century. We may not set up the judgments of any one century as infallible, certainly not those of a century so disappointing as was the fifteenth century in England. Dryden and many others since have reversed the judgment of the fifteenth century regarding the *Canterbury Tales*. But each reader is required to make afresh his own judgment. The *Canterbury Tales*—even in the fragmentary state in which the planned whole was left—seems to me the fulfilment and crown of all Chaucer's poetry inclusive even of *Troilus and Criseyde*.

It is possible to see why fifteenth-century readers—as, perhaps, Chaucer's own contemporary audience before them—might find *Troilus and Criseyde* more familiar than the *Canterbury Tales*, as on the contrary modern readers have found the latter more familiar than the former. Chaucer begins by working in conventions which would be well understood by his audience and which would be common ground. As he develops his art in these conventions he is, however, at the same time re-examining, criticizing and reshaping them. Certain of these conventions would be more obvious to a fifteenth-century reader in *Troilus and Criseyde* than in the *Canterbury Tales* and, perhaps, more acceptable than the new, daring and unfamiliar criticism of them which is nevertheless also present in *Troilus and Criseyde*. The new inventions of an author are always likely to be the last to be wholly accepted. It is in the *Canterbury Tales* that Chaucer's fertility of inventiveness attains its maximum.

In making this point, however, the last thing I wish is to seem to identify myself with a modern tone of amused superiority to Chaucer's England as 'simple' in the sense of 'primitive'. No one who has really tried to read Chaucer's poetry as what it is could adopt that tone. It is a poetry which implies a whole society, and that society is such that our own does not seem obviously superior in the comparison. The 'simplicity' of Chaucer's poetry is in fact complex and genuinely sophisticated by comparison with our modern complicatedness and the pretences which often go under the name of 'sophistication'. It is a poetry which evidently expects its audience to recognize the soundness and rightness of the most delicate moral judgments. A society which could be expected to be made thus sensitively aware of what is evil in itself is a profoundly healthy society.

Chaucer's subject—the subject which is present in the poetry that renders it and which, therefore, we do not need to search for outside the poetry—is human nature, human nature observed as particular persons in a particular society planted in Nature and in God. The poetry of Chaucer expresses a complete and glad acceptance of life, involving the acceptance of full moral responsibilities; it involves very sensitive and sure ethical discriminations and judgments. That unreserved acceptance of life does not (as has been too easily supposed) imply moral complacency; Chaucer's poetry is a most delicate evaluation of life. If he is not a 'moralist' as Dante is, his poetry is profoundly moral and profoundly religious in a Lawrentian sense (if one thinks again of the opening of the *Canterbury Tales*).

Though life is realized as bountiful and rich in the *Canterbury Tales*, the poet, we may agree, is beginning to look back on it and there is often a tone of disenchantment and even of what some might call disillusion. But it is a disenchantment with enchantments not with life, a disillusion with illusions and these are false things ('fantasye'). It is, rather, a clarity of self-knowledge attained at the summit of Chaucer's art and life.

The nearest equivalent to a late eighteenth-century Chaucer is Crabbe, that other master of the verse *nouvelle* in English. There is the passage in the *Village* that corresponds to—yet contrasts with—the opening of the *Canterbury Tales*. This passage, like the opening of the *Canterbury*

Tales and of Eliot's *Waste Land*, is a key to what the poet is going to offer us, communicating in carefully chosen, though also deeply felt, symbols a vision of life, the poet's view of the relation between man and Nature which the subsequent Tales exemplify.

> Lo! where the heath, with withering brake grown
>   o'er,
> Lends the light turf that warms the neighbouring
>   poor;
> From thence a length of burning sand appears,
> Where the thin harvest waves its wither'd ears;
> Rank weeds, that every art and care defy,
> Reign o'er the land, and rob the blighted rye:
> There thistles stretch their prickly arms afar,
> And to the ragged infant threaten war;
> There poppies, nodding, mock the hope of toil;
> There the blue bugloss paints the sterile soil;
> Hardy and high, above the slender sheaf,
> The slimy mallow waves her silky leaf;
> O'er the young shoot the charlock throws a shade,
> And clasping tares cling round the sickly blade;
> With mingled tints the rocky coasts abound,
> And a sad splendour vainly shines around.

This poetry is an earnest of Crabbe's sympathy for the plight of the country folk of his day. In contrast to Chaucer's feeling of the bountiful Nature of which man is unconsciously part, Crabbe saw that in his time and place there was a losing struggle for existence, man's endeavours to scrape a living, like his aspirations, being 'blighted', 'mocked', 'withered' and choked by weeds. But the poet feels the pathos of the struggle and distils his feeling in the last line—there *is* a 'splendour' which 'shines around' 'the rocky coasts' that man's lot is cast on, it is the fact that the struggle continues even against such odds; but the splendour is 'sad' because it does not help the sufferers, it *'vainly* shines'. The buoyant sense of well-being that characterizes Chaucer's poetry is replaced by Crabbe's compassion, acquiescence by indignation. Crabbe's wit (like Jane Austen's) is his eighteenth-century equivalent of Chaucer's wit. But beneath his liveliness there is a moral seriousness and a sceptical melancholy which associates him not only with Jane Austen but also with Samuel Johnson; it is his eighteenth-century equivalent of Chaucer's mediaeval gravity.

2

Our object is the poetry of Chaucer—the object which alone may be said to exist in the present. Chaucer the man has perished together with the whole society in which Chaucer the man lived. Nevertheless, that society is implied in the poetry; and in the ways in which it is implied —as it has been caught up and transmuted in the poetry— it remains immediately apprehensible. It is implied also in the poetry of Chaucer's English contemporaries. Chaucer is no isolated genius. His poetry implies a cultivated audience and is such as would lead us to expect that there were other cultivated poets among his contemporaries. It is what we do find—and I am not thinking only of Gower. Indeed, what we might scarcely be prepared for, even by the reading of Chaucer's remarkably various poetry, is the wealth and variety of the sophisticated poetry of his English contemporaries when we take the trouble to begin to investigate it as what it is—poetry. That it has been generally classified as unsophisticated and naïve is a reflection on the literary naïveté of modern scholarship. Its sophistication often turns out to be simply of a different kind from the standard French kind. But what is evidence of a wide and rich English mediaeval civilization is the number of widely different English poems that are contemporary with Chaucer's—poems widely different both from Chaucer's and from one another—many of them apparently accidental survivors from among a much greater number of poems. English mediaeval society could evidently provide audiences capable of responding to complex poetry by accomplished poets belonging to different schools and traditions. The audiences implied by these diverse poems are evidently not identical but have so much in common, so over-lap and are inter-related that they build up into one richly diverse, yet integrated audience— the total audience there was for the art of poetry in England in Chaucer's time. Only a series of literary critical studies of individual poems could establish this as a fact that might be generally accepted, and that is beyond the scope of a book which is specifically a study of Chaucer's poetry. But perhaps no study of Chaucer's poetry should end without at least a recognition of the rich and varied and humane English civilization implied both in Chaucer's poetry and in the poetry of his English contemporaries.

For Chaucer is, of course, the end and climax of a social culture and a literary tradition, their fine flower—as well as the originator of later literary work. After all, the Middle Ages were on their last lap when Chaucer was composing the *Canterbury Tales*, and indeed he could not have produced so fine and sophisticated an art except as the final outcome of a long evolution. As Miss Phillpotts concludes when tracing the literary descent of the Sagas, 'Great literature is no catch crop'. Her admirable analysis of the literary and social and anthropological history of the Eddic poems and the Sagas[1] provides a model for the kind of history of our English mediaeval literature that we so badly need. Such poems as Chaucer's and Langland's, *Sir Gawayn and the Grene Knight* and the Ballads with their conventions, their symbolic uses of language and various metrical systems and literary idioms, must have had a long tradition—a history that needs disentangling and charting—of practice by poets and comprehension by audiences educated in responding to poetry.

Professor Raleigh's remark that Chaucer did not himself create the language in which he composed needs to be

[1] In *Edda and Saga* and *The Elder Edda and Ancient Scandinavian Drama*.

extended to include the other varieties of English in which Langland, the poet of *Sir Gawayn and the Grene Knight*, and so many other poets composed. The mediaeval English people had been for at least two centuries shaping these rich local varieties of English in their talk; and they provided the audiences for the different poems in these varieties of English. One of these audiences could be expected to respond to poems as different from one another as Chaucer's *Hous of Fame*, *Troilus and Criseyde*, *The Man of Law's Tale* and *The Nonne Preestes Tale*. Another of these audiences—not necessarily so entirely distinct from Chaucer's audience as has been assumed—could respond to the very different and very complex poem of *Piers Plowman*.

Piers Plowman has been found confusing by modern readers. The more one grows into that poem, however, the less certain will one become that that is the poem's fault. It is more likely that it has become too difficult to keep clear the distinction between the different kinds of meaning that are often simultaneously present at any one point in the poem and to recognize their relation to the developing total significance. The mind is required to move on two or more planes of meaning at the same time without confusing them and to be alert to an interplay of developing significances.

There is in one of the earlier *passus* of the poem (to recall a comparatively simple instance) a paragraph which is both a realistic impression of one of Edward III's winter campaigns and also allegory. Conscience is visualized by his accuser, Lady Meed, first as a private soldier shrinking from the cold, hungry, and fearful for his life; then as a pillager bearing on his back towards Calais a bag of brass to sell. Evidently Langland's audience could be relied upon—as a modern editor of the poem cannot—not to confuse the images with their allegorical significance. The bag of brass is literally pillage but allegorically money which Edward, troubled in mind because of the sufferings of his army, accepted as compensation for abandoning

French provinces and withdrawing to Calais. If these two planes of meaning become entangled—as they can so easily become if one is not accustomed to this kind of poetry—the passage falls into confusion. By visualizing Conscience as a cowardly soldier and a pillager Lady Meed is trying to discredit him. The point required to be understood by the audience is that Lady Meed only discredits herself by her slander of Conscience. A virtuous person may be slandered but not a virtue; Conscience 'is as the air invulnerable' and Lady Meed's slanders 'malicious mockery'.

But the reader who is responding to the realism of the satiric element in *Piers Plowman* and is at the same time fully aware of the allegorical significances has to make a further more radical adjustment in responding to the symbolism of the mystical element as that develops, particularly in the later *passus*. The meaning which emerges on this different plane is in fact the central or innermost meaning; yet it is the meaning which has been least attended to by modern readers who have often read the poem merely for the evidence it contains about social conditions in the fourteenth century.

The 'characters' (to recall simply the 'characters' from the complex poem) move together with the rest of the meaning on the several different planes. Some are persons, others are personifications or allegorical figures, others are symbolical figures. Most of the characters, indeed, move on more than one of these planes at once. The allegorical characters—the most vividly realistic of these being, perhaps, the Seven Deadly Sins in *passus* V—require a kind of response that is not dissimilar to that which is appropriate to Ben Jonson's art. On the other hand, Haukyn the Waferman—on the naturalistic plane a familiar character of the fourteenth-century London streets—accumulates and develops a rich and complex symbolical significance. Piers himself—the Plowman—moves on different planes simultaneously and means something more with each successive reappearance. He grows in his developing context into an ever more rich and complex symbol—the central symbol of the poem.[1]

Surely, therefore, it will not do to persist in regarding *Piers Plowman* as implying a primitive audience. Even the more purely doctrinal passages—which may too easily be dismissed by modern readers as not 'poetry'—are anything but child's play. If *Piers Plowman* is the 'popular' poem it has been taken to be—and I would agree that there is a sense in which *Piers Plowman* is a great 'popular' work of art—it was evidently possible for a poem by one of Chaucer's contemporaries to be both 'popular' and complex art.

The audience for poems in the alliterative tradition in which *Piers Plowman* belongs must have been no less experienced and expert in responding to poetry than was the audience for those different poems the conventions of which were adapted from *Le Roman de la Rose* and the French romances, assuming that these two kinds of audience were distinct. But there are reasons for doubting whether these two audiences were in fact so mutually exclusive and isolated from one another as we assume them to have been, whether one and the same person might

[1] The popular comprehension of the symbol is proved by the numerous wall-paintings in English mediaeval churches of Christ as Piers Plowman, on which Professor Tristram, the authority on mediaeval wall-paintings, wrote a very interesting article ('*Piers Plowman* in English Wall-Painting') in *The Burlington Magazine* for October 1917. He says: 'Altogether there are fourteen or fifteen examples of wall-paintings in which this subject may be identified—a large number to have survived the vicissitudes of five centuries, and in itself a proof of its popularity. They are found scattered in counties as widely separated as Bucks, Suffolk, Berks, Sussex, Gloucestershire, Cornwall and Pembroke in Wales. The workmanship is generally unskilled and they are clearly paintings of the poor and not of the rich. Much the same may be said of the MSS. of the poem. Over thirty exist, all of which are of a poor type. The paintings are all later than the first version of the poem, and are clearly directly inspired by it.'

Incidentally, the variations in the MSS. of *Piers Plowman* seem to show that even some of the written literature was in the ballad-stage of being folk-handled and folk-formed.

not have been a member of both these audiences. That remarkably fine West Midland alliterative poem, *Winner and Wastour*, is the immediate predecessor—in the same tradition—of *Piers Plowman*. The debate between the two characters, Winner and Wastour, is the nearest thing to some of the episodes in *Piers Plowman*. Yet the setting— the scenery, the spectacle of the two armies in battle array, the resplendent royal pavilion—is a lively local variation of the conventional dream-vision settings of the French courtly poems and their English equivalents. The same element is to be found also in *Piers Plowman*. But *Winner and Wastour* is unmistakably intended for the ear of the King himself and of his counsellors. It deals with a delicate social and economic problem and proffers advice on statecraft—apparently to King Edward III himself—so boldly that it is evident the poet could feel that he counted in national affairs and expected to be listened to by the highest in the land. Chaucer's poetry was evidently intended to be listened to by the King and Queen and their Court. But this very different poem in a very different tradition—unmistakably an immediate predecessor of *Piers Plowman*—was evidently also intended to be listened to by the King and his Court. The alliterative poets of the West Midland dialects were conscious of their national function and their influence on the conduct of affairs in the kingdom, as the poets of the Kingdom of Scotland still were a century later.

The poet of *Winner and Wastour*—a poem intended for as noble an audience as, only a generation later, was Chaucer's very different poetry—is conscious that he belongs to an ancient and proud tradition of accomplished artists; he deplores the modern neglect of poets by the lords in favour of inexperienced and untalented minstrels.

Whylome were lordes in londe that loved in thaire hertis
To here makers of myrthes, that matirs couthe fynde,
Wyse wordes with-inn, that writen were never
Ne redde in no romance that ever renke herde.

Bot now a childe appon chere, with-owtten chyn-
   wedys,
That never wroghte thurgh witt three wordes
   to-gedire,
Fro he can jangle als a jaye, and japes can telle,
He schall be levede and lovede and lett of a while
Wele more than the man that makes hym-selven.
Bot never the lattere at the laste, when ledys bene
   knawen,
Werke witnesse will bere who wirche kane beste.

That the poets of the fourteenth century could depend on
audiences skilled in the interpretation of poetry should not
surprise us. The good custom of providing an audience in
hall after dinner and hospitality for the wandering poet
had been long established. The chivalrous society had inherited the custom from the heroic society. Since the
poems were recitative and the dialogues would be enacted,
it is also not surprising that the poetry of the fourteenth
century has a pronounced dramatic character.[1]

Towards the end of his valuable *English Literature from
the Norman Conquest to Chaucer* Schofield remarks on how
many of the Middle English poems (including *Sir Gawayn
and the Grene Knight*) 'exist in unique manuscripts or not at
all in their original forms'. But he does not draw the
obvious conclusion that, if so much of what we have has
been preserved by accident, much more must be assumed
to have perished, and that the poems which we do have
are the evidences of an *unbroken* tradition of poetic art in
each of their particular dialects. He goes on, however, to
note:

'When the Saxons gained dominion in the land, they

[1] From their consideration of another oral literature, that of Iceland,
Miss Phillpotts and W. P. Ker argue that, being a social function, oral
literature is inevitably a collaboration between author and audience; but
though it must be popular (otherwise it would not be kept alive, once
the early ritual sanction and uses had disappeared), yet it is popular in no
derogatory sense. Its influence, on the contrary, is educational since it
brings about a *levelling-up* of interests and culture.

brought with them the tales they had been accustomed to hear at home, some at least of which were in literary form. Unfortunately most of these have disappeared even in their early alliterative dress, and none at all are preserved in mediaeval redactions. A mythical story of the Germanic hero Wade, father of great Wayland the Smith, and of his magic boat, is several times referred to by Chaucer and other Middle English writers, but we are now ignorant of its substance, despite the recent discovery of the scrap of an old poem on the subject.'

Chaucer's audience of courtly folk evidently listened to traditional Germanic tales as well as to French romances.

He song; she pleyde; he tolde tale of Wade.

It seems unlikely that they, and their predecessors for generations back, did not listen to these tales, at least occasionally in the traditional alliterative form; unlikely that the tradition of alliterative poetry was carried on throughout the Norman-French period only among the unsophisticated.

We cannot suppose that English alliterative poetry could suddenly have burgeoned afresh in the fourteenth century in the West Midlands into such a superb masterpiece of sophisticated art as *Sir Gawayn and the Grene Knight* unless there was in that locality a living tradition of such poetry with its roots deep in the past. The fourteenth-century alliterative poems of the West Midlands do not at all look like the work of a self-conscious archaic revival. Schools of poetry—implying both a public for that particular kind of poetry and a succession of skilled poets—*must* have continued the practice of the art in alliterative verse in both the North- and South-west Midlands. We simply have a break in the records till the fourteenth century. Even such a masterpiece as is *Sir Gawayn and the Grene Knight* has been precariously preserved on only a single manuscript. If *Piers Plowman* had not been popular enough to be preserved in many MSS., we should not even have known of Langland's existence, since there are no references to him other than those in his poem.

Mr. H. S. Bennett remarks somewhere that even if Chaucer had chanced to see *Sir Gawayn and the Grene Knight* in manuscript he might not have been able to understand it because of the dialect.[1] The assumption is that we enjoy such advantages over Chaucer that we can understand a poem by one of Chaucer's own English contemporaries which he himself could not have understood. But, if Chaucer could understand poems in other languages, why should he not have been able to understand poems in English dialects other than his own metropolitan English? There seems no doubt that *Piers Plowman* was read in London, though evidently composed (probably also in London) by a man of the South-west Midlands in substantially his own dialect. There seems little more reason to doubt that *Sir Gawayn and the Grene Knight* could also have been understood in London. Fourteenth-century London must have been full of soldiers, clerics and craftsmen from all over England. Is it likely that the nobles of the North-west Midlands (who must have formed an important part of the audience for such poems as *Sir Gawayn and the Grene Knight*) were not familiar enough visitors to the Royal Court? It is arguable that the mediaeval English dialects were *less* different from one another than are (if written down phonetically) the modern dialects of Essex, Devon, Cornwall, Lancashire or Cumberland. There must have been tremendous scribal activity, both clerical and lay, for only a fraction of their copies can be reasonably supposed to have survived; and the scribes, we know, were able and apt to change a text from its original form into the dialect of their own community; there are also 'border-line' cases of texts in intermediate forms, for dialects in practice were not the water-

---

[1] *Chaucer and the Fifteenth Century*, page 10. 'We have no evidence whatsoever that works such as *Pearl* and *Sir Gawain and the Green Knight* ever came his way, or that he could have coped with their difficult dialectal peculiarities even had they done so.'

tight compartments of the text-books but, being living speech, must have blended and must have shaded off from one another by degrees. The people throughout the length and breadth of England in Chaucer's time must have had much in common; the traditional pattern of their lives must, for all its rich local variations, have been essentially one; they were everywhere engaged in agriculture, crafts and market-town occupations, and they were all members of the one mediaeval Catholic Church. Robert Henryson in Scotland had evidently no difficulty in reading and enjoying Chaucer.

Richly local as *Sir Gawayn and the Grene Knight*[1] is there is nothing provincial in a limiting sense about it; it is in the best sense sophisticated. It implies, as Chaucer's poetry does, a cultivated audience, and it implies that—contemporary with Chaucer's metropolitan audience—there was such an audience in the North-west Midlands, a region comparatively remote from the metropolis. This sophistication is not of the kind that could have been acquired merely by familiarity with French courtly romances. We are wasting our time if we try to fit *Sir Gawayn and the Grene Knight* into the familiar category of French Romance. This poem in the radically different English alliterative tradition is complex and richly significant art, sophisticated and popular, realistic and symbolical, courtly and pre-courtly, Christian and pre-Christian, rooted in an ancient and still a life-giving mythology, a Celtic nature-ritual that almost certainly persisted in that region through the Christian centuries. Its complexity is matched by its completeness as a single work of art. The poem is the crown, the masterpiece (among the group of poems of the North-west Midlands which have been accidentally preserved[2]) of what was evidently a whole school of poetry

[1] The reader may be referred to my essay on *Sir Gawayn and the Grene Knight* in *Scrutiny* (Winter 1949) for a fuller account than can be offered here.

[2] They include *The Auntyrs of Arthure at the Tarn Wadling* and the alliterative *Morte Arthure*.

that flourished in the same region. Even *The Pearl*, that unusually fine North-west Midland dream-vision poem, happily preserved in the same unique manuscript as *Sir Gawayn and the Grene Knight*, is very different from the dream-visions of the French allegories of courtly love which were among Chaucer's models. Yet it is not less 'courtly' than they are.

Of the Miracle Plays which, performed annually, were a vivid feature of town life in Chaucer's time the only complete cycles which have been preserved—the Chester, York and Townely (probably Wakefield) Plays—happen also to be Northern. There was at least one dramatic poet of genius in that region—the author of the two Townely Shepherds' Plays, a substantial part of the Play of the Last Judgment and other parts of the Townely Cycle. Is it likely that he was an isolated case of genius receiving no comprehending co-operation from his community?

Innumerable lyrics—words for song—must have perished. The various lyrics we do have are evidently only stray survivors. Yet they imply again, as Chaucer's poetry does, the mediaeval English organic community. The lyrics 'Lenten is come with love to toun' and 'Bytuene Mershe ant Averil', for example, have the closest relation to the opening of the *Canterbury Tales*. It is a community dissociated neither from nature nor from its past. The specifically Christian carols can be shown to be rooted in pre-Christian fertility ritual. The lyrics evidently originated as words for the songs and dances of the seasonal festivals and they are still in the fourteenth century—as often as not—words intended for music. The art of music both for groups of voices and of instruments was (we know) highly developed in Chaucer's time. But to review the various other arts which in addition to the art of poetry flourished in England at that time is beyond the scope of a study of Chaucer. A comprehensive review would (I believe) establish that, corresponding to the varied public there was for the art of poetry in Chaucer's England, there must have been as varied a public responsive to—indeed actively sharing in—these various other arts and crafts.

But, quite apart from the evidence of the other arts, the poetry alone implies wide and strong and deep-rooted traditions alive throughout England in Chaucer's time. The people, in their different social, cultural and regional strata, were integrated in a living relationship—composed a single civilization. Chaucer's poetry and that of his English contemporaries is the evidence that there was throughout England a vivid and varied local life in touch with the metropolis and Europe.

A vast international background is implied in the national and local poetry. It is, indeed, in and through the various national languages and local dialects that the mediaeval European literary tradition lived. England shared fully in the life and traditions of Europe. The literatures of mediaeval Europe, when viewed comparatively and realized as a single complex whole, themselves provide all the evidence we need of how free were the channels of communication not only for the exchange of ideas but for the exchange of themes and poetic conventions. Tales, for example, must have been carried in very little time from the Mediterranean to all round the Baltic and the Atlantic seaboard. Between *langue d'oc*, *langue d'oil*, Italian, German, Scandinavian and English there was evidently a continual interchange of themes and poetic conventions. Differences of language and dialect could not have isolated the poets and their publics from one another's poetry. The poets themselves were the medium of this continual interchange. The traditional Celtic tales, for example, were re-cast by the poets in their own diverse languages and dialects. There was thus a vivifying interplay between the traditions.

What Chaucer did with the literary 'sources' he worked on—what he did with *Il Filostrato*, for example—needs to be considered in relation to what the other mediaeval English poets did with their literary 'sources'. The differences between the English versions and the French—in the cases where there *are* French and English versions—show distinctly that there was an English sensibility. This distinctively English sensibility is developed in the poetry of Chaucer and his English contemporaries. These English poets point straight to Shakespeare in ways which are implied in their using what is essentially the same language as Shakespeare.

We may indeed claim that Chaucer's poetry and that of his English contemporaries are, for all their range, integrated; and therefore imply a single complex civilization. Is Dante's Italian town civilization obviously richer or more humane than that implied by Chaucer's English poetry? Is the background of life—civilized life—implied in Dante's poetry obviously more wide, full and varied than that implied in Chaucer's poetry? Is it, perhaps, the contrary? We assume too easily the superiority of French and Italian mediaeval civilization. We have certainly no right to do so while English mediaeval poetry remains comparatively neglected. Could a French poet have made anything so rich and humane of the Bird and Beast Fable as Chaucer made of it in the *Nonne Preestes Tale*? Is it easy to find another mediaeval European poet of such large and deep humanity as Chaucer?

INDEX

219

220

221